DRIVING WITH THE BRAKES ON

HOW TO RECOGNIZE AND RENOVATE THOUGHT STRUCTURES WE CREATE THAT STEER US OFF OUR PATHS

WILLIAM A. MURPHY

High Mesa, LLC

P.O. Box 681, Cornville, Arizona 86325
Driving with the Brakes On: How to Recognize and Renovate Thought
Structures We Create That Steer Us Off Our Paths

Published in the United States by High Mesa LLC via Lightning Source, a
subsidiary of Ingram Press. High Mesa LLC books are available through
Ingram Press, and available for order through Ingram Press catalogues.

The author of this book does not dispense medical advice or prescribe any
treatments or techniques mentioned in this book. The intent of the author
is only to offer information to help the reader in their quest for spiritual
understanding and to help them on their life's journey. It is the right of the
reader to use or not use the information in this book. In the event the reader
uses this information the author and the publisher assume no responsibility for
the reader's actions.

Library of Congress Cataloging-in-Publication Data
Murphy, William A.

Driving with the brakes on: how to recognize and renovate
thought structures we create that steer us off our paths/
William A. Murphy
    ISBN   978-0-9849865-0-7   eBook
    ISBN   978-0-9849865-1-4   (trade paper)
    1. Consciousness, spirituality, intentionality
    First edition October 2012

Acknowledgements

I want to thank Lin, Tom Bird, Maggie C., Sue, Dad, Victoria, Rama, and all others in my life who were part of the experiences that have been listed in this book. You are all amazing, and I appreciate all of you. Thank you for helping me so much, believing in me, and providing the support needed to bring this book to fruition. Also thanks to any angels who have watched over me all those times when I was in danger. Please don't stray too far; I might not be done...

I also want to thank my editor, Thomas Hill, and the crew at Launchpad Press for helping me with this project. I appreciate all of you.

Cover artwork created by www.GoWildGrafix.com.

Disclaimer

The author of this book does not dispense medical, psychological, or financial advice and does not advocate exercises or examples in this book as a form of treatment for any physical or emotional issue or problem. This information is offered in good faith to assist readers in finding spiritual and emotional well-being for themselves. Readers have the right to use the information in this book and assume all responsibility for their actions and their lives.

Contents

INTRODUCTION

This is not a scientific journal trying to prove anything or convince. It is intended to be a catalyst for us to expand our thoughts, concepts, and questions about what is possible, what actually exists, and what is an illusion. We have been taught to rule many things out, to disregard perceptions outside the five senses lest we be considered weird, unbalanced, or other such labels. We can rethink what's possible. The things in this book have happened. Many times the beliefs we've become comfortable with don't easily allow the expansion of our thoughts and abilities beyond what our society deems "normal." This model is the exact thing restricting us from considering broader possibilities and perceptions. There are fantastic things that have happened and are happening all the time. You can expand your viewpoint of what's possible, reach into those areas you are curious about, and do some reading about them. This will stretch your boundaries.

We frequently become tightly defined by our environments, material possessions, education, or family. But what if all that was incidental and contained a significant amount of misdirection and untruth? There are several main intentions of this book, and one of the first is to invite you to look beyond this physical plane and reconnect to your essence. It is an invitation to expand our concepts of who we are and where we're going.

The next part of this book will show how we are being steered in our daily lives and how we set up thought patterns that continue to steer us along paths we may not have selected. We can also be unaware that we are doing this or how these things came to be. This concept called "thought structures" lays out how we can easily wind up "driving with the brakes on" in our lives, hence the title.

The thought structures concept will be woven throughout the book to give examples of these and how we can see them as they begin to happen. This makes it less likely we will become steered onto paths we don't want as we go forward into our futures. We will see how we have set out on our own courses or paths in ways that may be entirely off what we had originally intended when we came into physical form.

Next we will explore what science has discovered about how decisions and beliefs we create affect us and others on both microcosmic and macrocosmic levels. We will also look at how different types of energies and communications can impact the way in which we evolve on our life's path.

Finally we will examine a few ways to get back on track and become more aligned with where we want to go, who we want to be, and become aware of how to get there. It's a book about our voyage in the physical and how we can get more out of it.

Let's start with this truth: you are sacred and have incredible value.

SECTION 1:

ORIENTATION TO
THE SPIRIT

CHAPTER 1
OUR SPIRITUAL ESSENCE

Beginnings

I remember coming to this planet for this lifetime. I didn't remember this whole thing until much later in life. One day I just recalled it in its entirety. I recall seeing myself approach the Earth from far away, an awareness of traveling through space. I was totally cognizant of this and my plan to become physical again. I remember seeing my parents. Then, as a small child, the memories of arriving here faded as the necessities of physical life and the demands of parents obscured the memory of my origins.

In the grand scheme of things, since there really is no death, everything just continues forward. Looking at it this way maintains the larger view, helping us all create a more meaningful life. The fact of the matter is you can be or do anything you can conceive of. You have everything it takes to be great. In fact, you are great already. Maybe you don't feel that way, but you are. All the wisdom needed concerning you and your path is within you. All the information is there. Many of the ideas in this book may seem different to you; then again they might feel somewhat familiar. Either way, my intent is to remind you of what abilities you have. Sometimes we have a tendency to steer ourselves away from where we want to go. However, we have frequent "help" from a variety of factors in our society in being steered away from our inner compass, so it's easy to get off track. To cultivate constant awareness of who we are, who we can be, and how to help ourselves get there, is the intent of this book.

We are light beings here in physical form—souls in the material world. We have always been here or somewhere else in one form or another. Consciousness and memories this life are retained on a deeper level for the next life. It is possible to remember earlier lives, but usually we don't in everyday experience. We may periodically remember or sense traces of an earlier life. Sometimes we experience a knowing that we have been somewhere or known someone during another time. We can experience a familiarity in some environments and have lengthy memories of being there at some other time. I know more than one person who recalled roads and scenery they were driving through, describing what was around the next bend, even though they had never been in that particular location physically in this current lifetime. Hypnosis and other techniques have been used in helping people to remember earlier lifetimes. Edgar Cayce is well known for making predictions and communicating with other lifetimes while under hypnosis.

We are going through lives as Earth and the planets go

through time. Each day is filled with momentary things, but the greater picture is about where we and the universe are going. It's not about where we have been. That has become information and experience. We are on a continuous path. Our journeys, and the overall journey of the universe, occur simultaneously. We are evolving as spirits, just as the mountains, streams, and land masses evolved by time experience, through interaction with other beings and other energies.

There is energy everywhere. We are composed of it, we contribute to it—and it to us—as it flows through us. It is awareness and experience. Energy recycles and continues, often changing into a different form. When a person or an animal dies, the life energy or spirit continues on, and eventually returns to the physical—bringing back what it has learned to the next life. This is the form of knowingness. This continues on and on through time.

There is no death, only transformation of state. As souls we continue to shift over time. We are shaped and changed as we experience more. Our essence is the same; there are the same elements and the same energies, but we are constantly evolving. So, if death, loss, or "tragic" consequences happen, it is all part of the expansion, all part of the evolution of our universe. All is remembered and all moves forward. The experience is continued, the universe remembers, and we remember deep in our souls.

As humans in a highly developed world, many of us have tended to interact much more extensively with each other than with nature or the cosmos, even though we are part of both. This is to our detriment. Life here is not without interference or interaction from other planetary races, influences, and other beings. Yet we all are progressing through time—each of us on our own journey, albeit together with others, simultaneously.

The mountains evolve, driven up from upheavals in the Earth's crust, and then shaped by the elements through time. It takes millions or even billions of years for their form to develop. In fact, mountains are always in flux—constantly changing, just as we are. We have awareness and abilities to perceive far beyond our five senses, yet we have frequently deprived ourselves of this potentiality by accepting the limiting beliefs forwarded in our society. As a result, we have experienced a lower development of ability than we should. All this has been part of our spiritual evolution. Though not optimum, it is still experience, and is bringing about more memory of the universe and building the data bank of the universe. We have many abilities we haven't allowed ourselves to experience. That is beginning to change. We can all tap into the divine because we are part of the divine, the part that helps it continue to discover itself and expand.

There is a data bank of all that has occurred in the universe called the Akashic records. The term *akasha* comes from a Sanskrit word that means "sky, space, or ether." The Akashic records are described as containing all the knowledge of human experience and the history of the cosmos.[1]

> The Akashic Records are understood to have existed since the beginning of The Creation and even before. Just as we have various specialty libraries (e.g., medical, law), there are said to exist various Akashic Records (e.g., human, animal, plant, mineral, etc.) encoding universal lore. Most writings refer to the Akashic Records in the area of human experience, but it is understood that all phenomenal experience as well as transcendental knowledge is encoded therein.[2]

In this time, we as humanity are beginning to awaken from a state of unconsciousness, and the energy in the universe is helping this happen. We have more tolerance and awareness of experiences involving spirituality. Recent work in quantum physics has opened ordinary awareness to the fact that there may be much more to us and our lives in physical form than previously thought. In general, many people have been searching for this type of data; there is a plethora of seminars, books, and movies addressing these subjects. With the celestial alignment that is occurring, we are physically receiving more light energy from the solar system. This is increased light energy coming to Earth, and is helping this awakening to occur.

As has been true throughout our history, those on the cutting edge of thought are often attacked or ridiculed for their unconventional beliefs. However, others follow in their footsteps, examine their beliefs, and add their own perceptions. The numbers of the aware are growing rapidly. Some are reaching out and bringing others along. This is a period of spiritual awakening and evolution unlike anything that has happened for a very long time. The number of books, movies, and TV shows dealing with spirituality, consciousness, and the origins of life has been on the increase for quite some time. The awareness of the significance of the year 2012 and all the attention it has garnered has caused an unprecedented amount of interest in who we are and where we are going. Values are changing for many of us as we move away from the acquisition of physical things as a priority.

All parts of the Earth are constantly evolving; yet, as we have established earlier, it is normally quite a slow process. You would be hard-pressed to see a change from year to year unless there was a volcano, fire, earthquake, flood, or other major event. As souls we are on a similar time frame. Considering that we and our universe are continually expanding, how much time would it take to experience all there is to experience? And new things to experience are being created all the time. Sometimes profound events can bring about a huge change in our perspective, personal desire, or necessity. These are the times we make faster progress on our path. We should be supportive of ourselves and others. Sometimes this seems impossible.

Being on our own path—learning, creating, experiencing, and getting our spiritual process straight—is the purpose of each life. Getting things straight and working through problems, letting things unfold, is what this universe does. It takes time, but there is nothing but time in this universe.

Animals and plants just do what instinct and their DNA tells them to do as they are born, grow, and die. When they are born no one tells them they have deficiencies, that they're not perfect, or are not well thought of. Neither are they taught they are superior or inferior to others in their kingdom, though some species may have natural fear of other species or compete with each other within their pack or group. This is why we can learn a great deal from being around animals if we pay attention. They are constantly in the moment and being themselves with no apologies. On the other hand, we are often busy putting problems and artificial time constraints in the way of everything we do.

I often wonder where my life would have gone had I not begun studying spirituality. This was a follow-up to my studies of religion in college— primarily looking at established religions. I became interested in learning more about my spiritual nature, origins, and potential in the 1970s. I began studying eastern religions, meditation, and other information I could find about the spirit. This search led me in many different directions. What I found were similarities in many concepts and these were the ideas closest to me as a spirit and resonated with me as most likely to be true. I began gaining more spiritual awareness and pursuing more spiritual studies as they became presented to me. I have been on this path since the late 1970s.

Connections

Of all that is going on in this universe, many of us are not aware of the connections between things. For instance, there is space everywhere and it is present in everything. Any object is mostly space. The appearance is of solidity, but that is not the actuality.

You may have heard the idea or the comments, "everything is connected" or "we are all connected." Let's explore this idea. What exactly is connection? There are many ways we can be connected, physically, spiritually, or psychologically. If you consider yourself dependent on someone, there is a connection. If you are afraid of something or someone, there is a connection to that energy that changes your behavior or your decision process. If you were out somewhere in the jungle and happen upon a large tiger, there would be a connection of sorts there. It would be a visual connection at first, but the energy between you would be perceivable by both of you, as perhaps fear; if you knew this particular animal, it could be something other than fear, perhaps recognition and a feeling of reunion.

But there would be a connection. You would be in each other's space, and there would be some sort of interaction between the two of you. Much of this would be outside the five senses of touch, sight, sound, smell, and taste.

Sometimes you may get a feeling or mental vision of what someone close to you is doing. Or you think of them and they call shortly thereafter. There have been times that I have actually received a vision of something happening with a friend or relative and later discovered it was correct. I believe it is an ability that can be improved. It is just perception outside the five senses. Even detectives may use psychics to help them gain insight into crimes that have occurred. These things can be perceived.

In another example, if a child could never please a parent or live up to his or her expectations, there would be connection and most likely an influence on the child's behavior—even after the death of the parent, and even after the child was an adult. This happens all the time. Emotional interaction is a connection of sorts, and it influences our perception and our thought processes. It can add to thought structures or rearrange them.

I have done many workshops in energy healing technology. In one workshop we did exercises where we learned how to cross barriers of time and space to perceive things at a distance as well as among those of us in the room. We practiced actually perceiving what was going on in another person by observing from within that person—seeing and feeling what was going on with them. Without going into how this was done, my point is that we do have the ability to perceive across "barriers" that are not really barriers to us as spirits and consciousness. These are abilities you can develop, and it strengthens the connection to our spiritual essence. Some of these technologies or practices are Mindscape (part of the BodyTalk System™), Matrix Energetics®, Emotional Freedom Technique (EFT), and many others. You can attend workshops or seminars and discover many things about yourself and others. These activities can increase the connection we have with ourselves and our environment. They will increase your perception.

We can be connected via family or social interests, a team, a town, church, or through common experiences. There are many ways. The point is these connections are real, yet we often do not consider them in this way. It is true that we are our own bodies and spirits, too, but there is a connection that is not commonly considered. We have all felt the influence on our emotional bodies of the laughing of a child, or of fear or violence. These types of events can be perceived by all present and even by those not physically present but there with attention. There have been times when I perceived a shift in my emotional body and found out later something had happened and I felt the same thing again. This is just perception and connection.

This would include circumstances like watching a game on TV and caring what goes on. Most people I have talked to have all felt momentum shifts, excitements, or deflations about what was happening. Have you ever felt the shift in energy when someone who looks extremely upset or angry enters a space? How could we perceive this if we were not somehow connected? Is this due to the existence of what is called the "ether"? As spirits, we have no limits to what we can perceive, except for the boundaries we construct due to our beliefs.

Exploring the concept of ether (from the Greek word *aither,* meaning "air") is fascinating. It has been defined, argued, and talked about in scientific circles since Ancient Greece. In his excellent book called *The Divine Matrix* (Hay House, 2008), author Gregg Braden notes that Sir Isaac Newton described ether as "an invisible substance that permeates the entire universe."[3] Newton believed it to be responsible for gravity and sensations of the body; he also considered it to be a living spirit. Many other scientists have discussed this phenomenon, and they make determinations about it through the years. It will undoubtedly continue. Something has made it possible for us to be connected to our world. This theme will also continue to weave its way throughout this book, and we will examine it in more depth soon.

Spiritual Experiences, Out-of-Body Experiences

If you get the idea that there really is no death, just a transformation from physical to non-physical, it is easier to let go of negative emotions connected to death and the loss of a loved one. Missing the physical part of them is what is difficult. We are not physical in totality; we do change form but do not cease to exist. There are various interpretations of this among different religions but, essentially, we are energy and consciousness. Energy and consciousness can change form but it does not cease to exist, and its essence does not change. Knowing this can be a tremendous outlook changer.

We are all on a path; it is ours, and we need to remember it is our path, despite the structure and people and society around us that tends to make us feel differently. While it is true that we are all in this together, is it more like our paths are co-located at various times and we are all joined by a common energy, but we are still on our own paths and need to remember that. We are consciousness. We continue through time. When people pass back into the non-physical state, they are still around, just in another place merely a veil away. You are capable of communicating with them and they can communicate with you—though it will be telepathic on their part. Feel it. Maybe it is just an impression or a feeling of love. Sometimes it may be more, like a sensation that is familiar, or actually things happening in the physical realm, such as lights going on, the feeling that the person is close, etc. It is usually very difficult emotionally when someone close passes away. When we are distraught, we may miss the subtle messages communicated to us. Keep this in mind, and try to quiet your mind at least for some time each day. Don't discount or dismiss what you perceive.

I had a very close relative who was a very spiritual person. She completely believed and understood the idea that there was no death—that she was a spirit moving through time and that she would remain herself after the death of her body. She had recently learned that she had an advanced stage of cancer, though she probably perceived things were not right months earlier. She did not want to go through treatment for it. She had decided she did not want to be a burden to anyone and did not want to continue with trying to survive in her lifetime given what she would have to go through. She expressed this openly to the family. She had basically decided it was time for her to depart; shortly after that she just collapsed. One of her daughters was there with her and called 9-1-1. The paramedics were able to restart her heart twice in the ambulance on the way to the hospital, but she never regained full consciousness. While still unconscious, she waited in the hospital long enough (a couple of days) for the whole family to arrive and say their good-byes. The whole family also believed that we as spirits leave the physical but eventually return again. Then she departed her body and passed into the next dimension, returning to non-physical form. Though she was non-physical, she was still around; we could all feel her there. It was a very peaceful feeling and she was there for us, so we could make the transition to life without her physical presence.

We all felt her presence distinctly for several days during the time of the funeral and for some time after. We would get thoughts of her, and feel things the way she had felt, her vibration was definitely there with all of us. After some time had passed, we had all become adjusted to her being gone from the physical. It seemed like she waited until we were all fine with it before she moved on. At times I still think of her and feel her presence. Souls have the ability to "check in" periodically and see how we are doing, and sometimes they do.

I have had other experiences where I clearly perceived another spirit and was able to communicate with it telepathically. One night when I was going to bed, I clearly heard my cell phone ring, but knew it was turned off. I got up and went to the kitchen and confirmed it was off. Upon arriving into the kitchen I felt a presence. The hair on the back of my neck stood up and I got goose bumps. It was not hostile but was not welcoming either; it was unfamiliar. I just stood there for some time and was receptive to its communication, but there was nothing really communicated other than to see if it could create an effect on me. I sent this presence the message that I could tell that it was there, and then sent it some affinity and appreciation. The energy in the space changed and it went away. It never came back. There have been numerous other times when I have perceived spirits. By just acknowledging them and sending them affinity, they usually moved on.

Another experience I had many years ago provided proof to me that I have perception and existence outside the body. I had been working outside all day in the heat. I was exhausted when I came home and it was very late. I was thirsty and drank a couple of beers. Shortly after that, I went to bed without eating. I was sleeping in the downstairs bedroom because we had young children and I needed to get up very early each morning for work. By sleeping downstairs I was less likely to awaken them and my wife so early. I needed to use the bathroom in the middle of the night, so I ran up the stairs. After arriving at the top of the stairs I felt light-headed. I passed out but did not realize I had done so. Within moments, my wife was up and I could see her; I heard her talking to someone on the phone. I could hear what she was saying, discerning that she was talking to 9-1-1, and I could hear the kids crying and wondered what was going on. I was "standing" right behind her and I could see nothing wrong. The only thing was my body was in the bathroom passed out! I was out in the hallway seeing and hearing my wife and hearing the kids but I was outside of my body. The combination of no food, beer, and running up the stairs had caused me to faint. But I had full perception. This experience was vivid and has stuck with me because it proved to me that perception exists outside the body and is independent of it. You will exist after the body is gone, just as you did before arriving in your present body.

I am always interested to learn whether people believe in ghosts. Ghosts, for the most part, are just people who are non-physical. They are spiritual energy and consciousness. If they are really stuck in an event and unable to move on, they may haunt a house or create some other effect, but they are just people who have returned to non-physical. Sometimes they may not even realize it. In some cases, they may not want to move on.

Have you ever had a spiritual experience, such as seeing yourself outside your body, feeling a strong sense of déjà vu, or getting an idea of something and then it happens? How about thinking of a person and they call or you run into them? When this happens oftentimes I hear someone say that is coincidence or spooky, when actually it was just a moment of heightened perception. These experiences can and should be normal. It is a feature of us being connected and having perceptual capabilities outside the physical body's limitations. We have this ability but may have a thought structure in place that tends to dismiss things like this as mere coincidence. Instead this is something that should be happening all the time.

The reason I bring all this up is to remind us that we are spiritual beings, we have abilities beyond what we have come to accept and/or consider "normal." It is sad that people who freely communicate this are thought of by many as a little weird or even mentally ill. I think about the movie, *The Sixth Sense*,[4] and what Joel, the main character who was a child, went through. In this movie he has an ability that he does not understand because he is young and it is frightening to him. He sees people who have recently died in a violent or unexpected manner. They don't know that they have died and they show up in his room or where he can see them. After he begins to understand this ability and what is going on, he is able to help these people and they don't scare him anymore. But, in the meantime, he cannot speak of this to anyone, as they think he is severely disturbed. He has perceptions outside what is considered normal or healthy, and it is unsafe for him to talk to anyone about it, even his mother. No one believes him, so he has to deal with it himself. It is both conceivable to me how this would play out in our world and realistic that he could have those abilities.

Another movie, *Dragonfly*,[5] with Kevin Costner, also has perceptions he and others in his environment have difficulty dealing with. In this movie, he is a doctor and has just lost his wife who was also a doctor. She worked with terminally ill children and had recently traveled to South America to provide volunteer medical help there. She never returns and his life is turned upside down. He begins experiencing paranormal phenomena he cannot explain and tries to dismiss these events like all the staff around him. It is as if she is trying to communicate to him. (She is!) Finally he ignores his own conventional thought structures and those of his peers. He realizes there is something going on he cannot ignore or explain and begins to follow his heart. He begins to pay attention, which leads to profound changes and actions that forever alter his perceptions and ideas about life.

Step one of realizing our potential is to first acknowledge that we can develop abilities and perceptions far beyond what is considered "normal." It's like we are stuck in this little game here on Earth and there are rules. If we start to bend them or disagree with them, we are ostracized, put on medication—or, worse, locked up. I believe this is changing; it is the conscious and aware ones who will change this viewpoint by learning new things and expanding and acknowledging concepts of what is possible. Consciousness is expanding among all of us.

CHAPTER 2
USING OUR SPIRITUAL ABILITIES

Visualization

There are many volumes written on visualization. Visualization is the technique of creating an image in your mind. Athletes do this all the time with their game plan, or to help them learn something new. It has been shown to be a tremendous supplement to practice. As a technique for creating things there is no question about the viability of visualization when used properly.

It is quite possible and often easy to visualize things you don't want. It works the same way. When you look around at man-made things in your environment, they all started out as a visualization in someone's mind first. You visualize yourself one way or another and create yourself as a result. I have worked with this for some time. It is a tool that can be tremendously helpful. I have had challenges with it many times, and I have also used it successfully. It is all in being aware of your mindset when you practice it, being aware of any habits you may have concerning about how you look at things. There have been plenty of times when I have looked at things with a negative viewpoint and through expectations without really realizing I was doing so. When continuing to do this, my expectations were realized regardless of being positive or negative. The beliefs underlying these visualizations matter! I will go into this in more detail shortly.

There's a great quote by Dr. Rob Gilbert, one of the world's leading experts on sports psychology. He says, "Losers visualize the penalties of failure; winners visualize the rewards of success."[1] Spending time visualizing success is a worthwhile activity. What's important to remember is what you think and know. This is what determines the path you will eventually find yourself on. Act upon your own beliefs. Things don't happen overnight. Sorting out these habits and formulating new ones takes time, effort, and realizing what you are doing to create your next chapters in life. I am writing from the viewpoint of having experienced these both positively and negatively and from seeing myself formulate my life. I am working on it constantly. Things have changed tremendously, and the fun is in seeing it become increasingly better and knowing I am getting help from the universe in making changes. I know that visualizing things eventually makes them happen, and I believe the universe is constructed to allow us to create in this way. I know this to be true because I have had it happen many times, including things I did not want to happen. The key is to be aware of what we are visualizing and creating.

Here's a story about visualizing. I was young and didn't

even realize what I was doing at the time. I was just visualizing something without thinking about how I could make it happen. I just wanted it to happen, knew someday it would, and let it go at that. Here's the story.

When I was growing up I wanted to ski more than anything else in the world. I was living in a place where there was limited skiing close by. My parents didn't ski, so there was not much time made for me to pursue it, since I was young and dependent upon them for transportation and money. I didn't get to go very often. I read the most popular skiing magazines. I kept every issue for years and would re-read them at night before going to sleep. I had re-read them so much that I managed to memorize extensive amounts of information about ski construction, ski resorts all over the United States, Canada, and Europe, as well as information and statistics about equipment, the personalities, etc. I spent countless hours in my mind, skiing down mountains and experiencing the freedom of that experience. I never tried to figure out how it would happen; I just wanted it and enjoyed the idea of it.

I did get to go on a couple of ski trips, including one with my church group and the YMCA, but they were few and far between. Finally, when I was in college, I had an opportunity to go to Jackson Hole, Wyoming, over a Christmas break. I went with some friends and decided to stay once I got out there. I dropped out of college over the phone, and got a job during the time I was out there, and just didn't return home! My parents totally freaked! I was finally able to focus on skiing and did so every day. I was in heaven! All I did was ski every day. I had a season pass and was able to work part-time and ski the rest of the time.

I was young and had not absorbed the "practical training in life" viewpoint. I had severely upset my parents. I had not thought through most of what I did, but I was doing what I had envisioned for many years, and that was all that mattered. Just being out there every day was the biggest creator of happiness I had ever experienced. This began a long change on my life path. But the important part is that I had visualized myself doing this for so long and now it was happening. I skied basically five days a week every season for the next eight years and wound up on the professional freestyle skiing tour that was in the early stages of formation. I skied like this until I decided to move into the next phase of my life, which was flying.

At the time, I did not realize all that visualization had helped me create the scenario. It was just something I had endlessly dreamed about without thinking through how it would be possible. I just knew someday, when I was old enough, that I would be able to make it happen and it did. I was not an adult looking for how to make it happen, it was just visualization with joy and imagination——no resistance to the idea. No practical, adult-oriented viewpoint of, "But how would that be possible?" It was done from pure joy with no effort to make it work out; it was just visualization over and over and then the opportunity presented itself. I made the leap. I have looked back at this experience many times in many different ways. It taught me a lot about myself, but also about how the universe works and how things unfold in the physical world. In our minds, they can unfold in an instant. But, with our experience pertaining to how things work in the real world, we can easily take the power out of our visualizations without realizing it. The universe works in miraculous ways.

Another Visualization Story

Many years ago when I was a flight instructor, I was in the process of trying to build flight hours to move up in my career, like most flight instructors do. I was not making much progress because the economy in 1981 was terrible and the aviation business was very slow. Several airlines had gone out of business, which put many highly experienced pilots back in the job market competing with me for positions. This was demoralizing for me because I was young and impatient. Often there would be nothing on my schedule, but I would have to be there in case somebody walked in and wanted a demo flight or lesson. Frequently I would have a student cancel. It was very disheartening. When this happened, I would go the sales department and get the keys to one of the many airplanes they had for sale. I usually picked one of two Beechcraft Barons. I would go down to the flight line and just sit in them and enjoy being in them, imagining how awesome it would be to fly one somewhere. I was qualified to fly them and the charter department used a couple of them. But I was not in the charter department yet, so I didn't get to fly them. Besides, with business the way it was, there were always other pilots available to fly them if the need arose. What was interesting about this in retrospect was the attitude I had when sitting in these airplanes. I wasn't unhappy about not flying them; I just sat there enjoying them, wanting and imagining what it would be like to be able to go somewhere in them with no students or charter clients—just me and the airplane—so I could purely enjoy the flight experience. I sat in these two specific airplanes frequently over a period of several months.

Here is the interesting development, though. During the

next several months, on three different occasions, I turned out to be the only available pilot to fly these same airplanes to different locations by myself: exactly what I had visualized. It was amazing and a total joy! One time I flew from Salt Lake City to Denver. On a different occasion I flew the other one from Salt Lake to Saint Paul, Minnesota. It was incredible. I was truly able to enjoy these flights, and it was totally the way circumstances lined up that made this happen. The universe works in mysterious ways! It winds up giving you what you are putting out there and not resisting. I was not resisting or feeling sorry that it wasn't happening; I was just enjoying being in these airplanes and visualizing me flying them. This was the same type of visualizing I did for skiing. It was not done from a viewpoint of lack, or wondering how or if it could happen. I just repeated visualizing having the experience and loving it.

Using times like this help me put together strings of good moments to refer back to, those which remind me of what can happen when I am creating moment to moment. Do this enough and you will find ways to revise your thought structures to include more positive and miraculous things. Practice and don't worry about when those things will come. Imagine how it would feel to be experiencing them now. We will touch on some pointers for improving your skills at visualizing later.

Difficult-to-Explain Phenomena

I had an experience when I was in the Boy Scouts on a camping trip. We were sleeping out under the stars. I clearly saw an object moving across the sky and making right-angle turns with no change in speed. It was far above the atmosphere where commercial jets fly. There is no way I can imagine it was anything from Earth. With how much evidence there has been on all aspects of extraterrestrial (ET) sightings and interactions with humans and the Earth, I find it impossible to believe all these accounts are false. Consider the Great Pyramids, the Nazca lines, the Bermuda Triangle, and numerous other sites around the world that are beyond an earthly explanation. I have revised my viewpoint and continually try not to exclude anything from initial consideration. There's too much we don't know about. Keeping an open mind about things increases your perception about what is possible. The truth is often so far outside what we normally think that it may not be believed. Many credible people tell us there are in fact many ET races among us and have been for a long time.

Of course, the existence of UFOs is still a highly contentious debate among some. Those contending UFOs exist have detractors. This is a great area of debate! I'm not going to spend much time covering this other than to consider the number of stars and planets we can see from planet Earth on a clear, dark night, especially in the clearer skies of the west, at altitudes well above sea level. How could anyone think there aren't other beings out there?! We can only see part of our galaxy, and there are more than 100 billion more galaxies projected to exist, depending on the source. That number of galaxies makes it highly likely there are many other worlds with life.

The point to this is that there are many things that evoke a sense of wonder. Also, it is important to realize that our world is changing. We are the ones changing it largely with our thoughts and awareness. If things get better, it will be because we as individuals raise and improve our individual consciousness and become increasingly aware of more possibilities.

Orbs and Other Phenomena

There are so many areas we know very little or nothing about yet. We are in a constant state of learning and discovery. That's our evolution. For example, there are phenomena in the environment that are often called orbs. No one I have found knows exactly what they are or why they are here. Explanations on what they are range from dust to energy sources, spiritually sentient beings to points of perception for some other civilizations from elsewhere. Orbs seem to be drawn to loving, positive energy. I have seen people attract them by having loving and playful energy. You can often see them at night by using digital cameras with a flash. Just take some pictures into the dark and see what's there.

There are many theories, but this is an area that can open up your sense of wonder and begin to change your thought habits and structures. I have taken many pictures of these phenomena and they are pretty interesting; there are different sizes and shapes, though most are round. I have seen some inside a friend's house when looking at pictures from a birthday party and others I have seen in my house at different times. Still others have been visible in pictures that I or my friends have taken while hiking at sacred places in the mountains. These have been visible in pictures taken during the day, though some of these look more like energy emanations than orbs.

There is a lot of information available on the Internet on these, and it is worth checking out to see what you think. There is a documentary film available, entitled *Orbs, The Veil is Lifting*,[2] that has a great deal of information on these phenomena. Some detractors contend that these phenomena are most likely dust or mold particles clustered together. It's quite possible that could explain some, but that does not explain the varied locations where I have seen them on photos I've taken.

One night a friend and I were taking pictures outside to see if there were orbs around. We found them in some parts of the yard but not others. There were some over part of the roof of the house, and over the lake, but not in other parts of the yard. We saw a few near some ducks that were sleeping by the lake. We have taken pictures in the house and seen them in some places, but then they were gone within the same hour. I have also seen other pictures taken by a friend that showed energy patterns far beyond those typical for orbs. These were taken by several different people in different locations and at different times of day. The "it's just dust" theory may explain some pictures, but it's not even close to explaining them all.

Angels and Others outside the Physical Realm Looking In

Back in the day, when I was skiing regularly, I dabbled in "recreational" substances and spent time in the bars at night with my peers. I have had some experiences that are noteworthy, which have confirmed my belief in guardian angels. I was coming home one winter night and should not have been driving. I lost track of quite a long span of time and "woke up," discovering that I was driving up a snowy canyon road with no recollection of how I got there. This was a winding road in the winter and somehow I hadn't driven home as planned. When I "woke up" I had no idea of where I was until I drove by a sign that told me. I had driven quite a long distance out of my way. At that point, I turned around to go home. There was no way I could have done that drive in my condition without help. For me to have safely navigated a narrow canyon road in a snow storm, unaware that I was even there, was not realistically something I could have done alone. Some being outside this realm was watching over me and made sure I was safe.

Here's another story where I consider a guardian angel was watching over me. I was piloting a cargo charter flight from Salt Lake City to a town on the other side of the Wasatch Mountains. It was a visual flight, not on instruments, because the weather was decent but with a high overcast. I took off and flew south to a canyon area where I could go through the mountains, make a course correction, and then proceed to my destination.

As I got through the canyon I could see the town I was flying to and it was being totally pounded by a huge and severe thunderstorm. There was lightning, hail, and a heavy rain shaft right over the airport. There was no way I would be able to land there. I was in an open valley so I began to circle in order to see if the storm would move off and allow me to complete the flight. Though the valley had good visibility, there was an overcast layer of clouds above. I was surrounded by mountains, all much higher than my altitude. I had space but not much. The only way out was the canyon I had just come through, and the destination that was out of the question.

Suddenly I perceived an urgent intuitive communication: "You need to get out of here right now via the canyon and get back into the valley; you are in danger." I immediately turned around and followed the instructions. As I exited the canyon into the valley, I looked back at where I had just been and it had completely turned into a cloud. Had I stayed even ten seconds longer, I would have been inside a cloud with zero visibility and much higher terrain all around me. Not a good situation. Looking back at this time—I have done this often—I believe I had an angel looking out for me again.

There will be more on angels later.

How the Universe Works (When We Let It)

There are countless stories of intervention such as these, and they are real. The point of this is there is much going on that is unseen, but it is not necessarily outside our capacity to perceive. Rather, it is outside of what the "normal" viewpoint is here on Earth. We just need to get more perceptive, look wider and deeper. Little by little we can increase our perceptions and begin to utilize them. Step one is becoming aware of them. Don't automatically dismiss things society tells us we should, lest we be labeled crazy. We will talk about how we are steered into thought structures and address detractors in the next section.

> "There are only two ways to live your life; one is as though nothing is a miracle. The other is as though everything is a miracle."[3]
>
> —ALBERT EINSTEIN

The universe will look out for us if we let it and acknowledge it. Of course, if you don't believe this, you will most certainly find confirmation of that. But developing the belief that the universe is looking out for you will be helpful. Here is an example of things working out in a pretty amazing way. Stories like these are plentiful.

A lady (I'll call her "Karen") had lost her husband of many years and continued missing him and living in sorrow long after his death. She could not let go. She joined a group of others who had lost their mates also. The group's function was to help participants work through their grief so they could move on with their lives. This process was not working for Karen. During that time she met Beth, also a recent widow. Beth had managed to pick up and move on with her life. They met each other in this group, got along fairly well, and developed a friendship. Karen had bought tickets to a cruise that she was planning to go on with her husband before he became ill. His illness progressed and he passed away, and she never went on the cruise. Since she did not go because of the circumstances, the cruise company held her reservation for a period of time. That time was running out and she was going to have to use the cruise credit or forfeit it. This had been the case for some time. She did not feel she could go by herself, but the deadline was approaching. A friend of Karen's suggested she ask Beth to go with her before she forfeited the trip. Karen decided this might be a good idea and asked Beth if she wanted to go with her. Beth said yes, and they booked a date before the expiration.

Karen and Beth had departed and were on the cruise; all was going well. There was a formal dinner night midway through the trip. Beth was excited to go but Karen had decided not to go because she did felt it would be too much for her, reminding her of the loss of her husband. Beth insisted she get dressed and go. Karen finally agreed and they went to the dinner.

They were seated at a table with several other people whom they did not know. They struck up a conversation with the people at their table. One couple at the table was there with their son. Karen discovered that this son knew an old high school sweetheart of hers named Stephen. Karen and Stephen had gone on to careers that took them away from their home city. Stephen had gotten married and involved in his life. Karen had also met someone else and become a wife and mother and proceeded with her life. Karen had more or less forgotten about Stephen but had always liked him. This son at the table had known Stephen for years as they had been working for the same organization in the same city.

He told Karen that Stephen had spoken of her several times through the years. Stephen had divorced and was living by himself. The whole time, another guest at the table (I will call her the "Angel") kept pressing the son about Stephen. "What has he been doing? Where is he now?" The Angel continued, persisting pretty much to the point of politely nagging. The Angel kept insisting that the son write down Karen's name and tell Stephen he had met Karen when he returned from the cruise. The Angel would not let up for some reason. If she had, the whole thing would have been dropped. The Angel really was an angel. They can come in all kinds of forms, I suppose, even a nagging and persistent individual!

The son also promised the Angel (and Karen) he would tell Stephen about their meeting at dinner. When the son returned from the cruise, he left a card on Stephen's desk saying "I met Karen, an old friend of yours." Stephen looked at the card and put it in his desk then promptly forgot about it. Nine months later he found the card and tried to find her but was unsuccessful. In the meantime Karen continued working through her grief and had begun to carry on with her life. It had taken some time. Shortly after that, Karen updated her information on her high school reunion website. Stephen thought he would try again, and this time he was able to find her and wrote her a letter. She called him and they wound up talking on the phone for hours. This was two and a half years later! Stephen had put the card away and simply forgot about it for all that time. Karen was just not ready. When she was everything fell into place. To jump to the ending of this story, they started seeing each other, and now are in love. They eventually got engaged and now are married!

Looking at this true story demonstrates how the universe can take care of you if you let it and trust that it will. Look at the probabilities of Karen finding Stephen and what occurred to bring this about and the series of synchronistic events: That *particular* cruise date after many had passed; Karen not planning to go to the formal dinner but being persuaded by Beth to get dressed and go; and then sitting at a table *out of all the possible tables among several huge dining rooms*, with a person who had the card of Karen's high school sweetheart—not to mention a totally unrelated person (the Angel) who was interested for some reason and who pushed hard enough on the son to make this thing happen. What are the odds of all that happening? The universe knows when the time is right and *it will look out for you*. Don't get in the way!

There are so many stories like this that happen all the time. Life is a miracle. Let it be so! Imagine if you learned to not only let it happen, but engage with it so that it can do more with you! There is a scene in *Star Wars: The Empire Strikes Back*[4] when Yoda has lifted Luke Skywalker's ship out of the swamp after Luke had failed in his attempt. Luke sees this happen and says in astonishment, "I don't believe it." Yoda responds with, "THAT is why you fail..."[5] Belief is powerful. Don't discount it. Learn to form it into what you want. The rest will follow if you allow it. Things may unfold differently than you had planned, but trust that it will work as you believe, because it will. We will delve more deeply into beliefs soon, including how they form and how to recreate them into something useful to you. There are many ways to do this.

SECTION 2:

THOUGHT STRUCTURES

CHAPTER 3
HOW WE APPLY THE BRAKES TO OURSELVES

Thought Structures

We are going to shift gears for a while with this next section. While we have the potential to experience and exercise higher perceptions, how come we often don't? How do we or did we get so far away from being who we really are? This section will get into why that is, and some of the reasons we developed habits that have brought us to where we may find ourselves. We can fix it.

Know this: We have infinite ability; we can tap into higher consciousness. We can perceive other dimensions and can see other things, but we're discouraged from doing so. We have forgotten how. We are primarily taught to think, not feel. There are rules, manners, etc. We may lose our ability to feel to the point of losing belief in ourselves. We are taught that certain things are "not real" and, if we persist in talking about them or perceiving them, we are in danger of being labeled and/or put on drugs, like so many children today. Perception outside the five senses is not very well acknowledged, nor is discussion of certain things.

As I was growing up, I bought into these limitations without realizing it. Being young and impressionable, I believed what my parents taught me, but they were the prototypes of their parents and the indoctrinations that had formed their lives. This is passed on and we just learn and believe what we are taught until we are old enough and brave enough to observe for ourselves. But oftentimes we don't look, so we continue to filter all experiences through these frameworks.

I want to cover how this concept of thought structures works. We'll define them then show all kinds of variations and influences on how they are formed, how we have been steered into believing certain things, operating in certain ways, and how ideas and beliefs expand and turn into thought structures. This section is in the book because I feel there is a level of awareness you can acquire that will not only help you dissolve things that are not helping you, but also give you tools to rebuild thought structures which will help you. Much of the time we don't pay attention to how we have constructed things. Knowing this will help us deconstruct paradigms that are not useful by seeing how we built them in the first place. This will also help us in the later sections to strengthen the new thought structures we will create. Being aware of how we created these patterns will be the tool to keep us from doing it on a continuing basis and wondering what's wrong.

After defining thought structures, we will explore them for a while and refer back to them occasionally. I will continue to weave this concept of thought structures throughout this book to show the many ways this concept occurs in our lives. Much of what we have come to know has to do with beliefs we have grown up with. Thought structures are ideas we have that define how we look at things that come along. They have beliefs as their foundation, much like the foundation of a building. The structure gets built up around the belief as time goes on. These structures can change at different places and along with different events in our lives. The universe itself changes as does our society—sometimes slowly and, at other times, more quickly.

Let's look a little closer at this concept of a thought structure. The dictionary defines "structure" as something built; anything composed of parts arranged together; the way parts are made or put together; and the relation of the parts or elements of a thing, especially as it determines its particular nature or character. Therefore, a thought structure is something built from various thoughts mostly connected in some way. This creates the whole structure of the idea: the character and nature of the structure.

We all have a pretty good idea what thoughts are. They are ideas, concepts, or notions formed in the mind: what one thinks, the process of coming up with ideas from mental activity or reasoning. These are filtered by what we believe to be true about something unless we are following a rigid discipline that is customary in scientific research. Even then, we most likely have an idea of what we are expecting to find from our research. Often we may not have examined why we believe it to be true.

A thought structure is a basic set of ideas that have each been received somewhere and have become beliefs. Then we build onto them by collecting more ideas that support the original idea.

It is like a house built onto a foundation. If the foundation is faulty, the house will not be sound either. The way to topple these foundations is to find a conflict related to it and see where the conflicts lead. This will usually show up with the dismissing of the data as unworkable or wrong. Examining this further will lead to a clarification of what the issues are, allowing you to begin the process of tearing it down and building one that is more beneficial to you.

I have found focusing on positive things and having positive affirmations is a great way to dismantle negative thought structures. When being positive becomes a regular habit, many of these thought structures will become visible, and you will suddenly see where some negative attitudes came from. You don't need to go back and try to undo them all. They will dissolve over time or be rendered null via positivity.

We tend to get an idea about something and then go about viewing our world through those reference points. Here's an example. Joe has an idea that flying is unsafe. He has no experience with aviation in particular except what he has read in the papers or seen on TV. Of course, the only time this happens is when there's a crash of some sort. That doesn't happen very often, so it really is news when it does. He looks at airplanes, especially small ones, as dangerous. He supposes that if the engine quits, the thing would just fall out of the sky. He is terrified every time he has to fly. He hasn't really thought of the fact that sailplanes or gliders fly for hours with no engine at all (i.e., the space shuttle when returning to Earth). He does not know how this would even work. He spends years hating the fact he has to fly for work and resists it. He might suffer anxiety and wind up on medication that can present a whole new set of problems. *Since he is resisting it by focusing on how much he hates it, he may find he has to fly for work more frequently.*

He then decides to be more positive about flying. Then one trip, he winds up sitting next to a flight instructor. As they talk, Joe brings up the fact that he has issues with flying. The flight instructor shows him how a wing creates lift. Then he shows him some other factors about what happens when that airplane turns, turbulence, the number of flights that occur each day with no incident, navigation, and so forth. Joe winds up understanding much more about flying. These new revelations begin to disassemble his negative and fearful ideas about flying.

We can easily build non-beneficial thought structures, and as a result put numerous barriers in our way. It is important to be able to see when that's happening. We need to see what's in the way, look within, and be totally honest with what we see there. It's usually an idea or pattern of thought. Even if there is something there that seems to be legitimate, an idea may have been there first and be underlying it. By being aware of this, we can sort things out and make desired changes in ourselves. We will discuss this idea at much greater length soon, but see if you can start noticing thought structures you may have as we continue. We may have built thought structures defining for ourselves what we are capable and not capable of perceiving.

'Reality-Based' Beginnings to Thought Structures

Thought structures often start with a "real" circumstance that's easy to simply adopt and build onto. For example, I was told at a rather young and impressionable age that I was not good in math. I had not been particularly *bad* at math until I got seriously behind one year. The reason for this was the fact that our school had become one of the first to begin the government experiment of busing kids across town. This resulted in a dramatic demographic change in our school population and was very disruptive. There were kids in my classes that actually assaulted teachers, threatened smaller kids to take their lunch money, and so on. I did not go into the bathrooms anymore except during gym class as they were mostly unsupervised, and it was unsafe. This was in junior high school.

I was living in a constant state of fear because, at the time, I was one of the smaller kids in my classes; the other reason was the viewpoint I was being raised with, one of scarcity and fear. This was fairly prevalent, and I just adopted these ideas as the way things were without examining them or deciding on them. They became part of my belief system. As a note, years later two of the students in my seventh and eighth grade math classes were convicted of armed robbery and served time in the state prison.

Needless to say, this was not a good environment for learning or asking questions, and I got behind. One teacher who was the head of the math department decided I needed to go into a different math class, one not as advanced. This was the origin and the reinforcement of my thought structure that I wasn't good at math. Of course, with math, everything is built on earlier concepts. If these concepts are not understood, it's difficult or impossible to follow what comes next. Not knowing this at the time, I just believed this foolishness about my own abilities and went with it. I began building this thought structure. The structure began with an idea first, which became a belief and went from there.

At that age, I did not critically examine the input and quality of teachers. On top of this, because of my "lower ability at math," certain types of careers were automatically ruled out for me, such as being a pilot, engineer, or other careers with heavy utilization and need for math skills. For years I believed this, and added to this thought structure accordingly. I don't bring this up to excuse anything; it's just to show how easily conclusions can be made that become reinforcing and life changing. This occurs because of someone's opinion, combined with my own belief in what I had been told. It is possible some of these evaluations are somewhat valid, but we need to examine them for ourselves before deciding. I've found many of my ideas came from such origins. I just accepted them as true at the time without really thinking about it.

Another Example of Thought Structure Formation

My grandmother was critical of my mother both as child and later as an adult. My grandmother was from the era that believed "children should be seen and not heard." This was the framework my mother grew up with. Though she formed her own ideas, they were built with this in mind. Her thought structures were constructed to filter things through a viewpoint that included other thoughts, such as:

"Watch your step."

"Others probably know more than you."

"Be careful."

"You can't always get what you want."

"Life isn't fair."

"Behave yourself."

"Don't get your hopes up."

"If you get divorced, you're a loser."

"Money doesn't grow on trees."

It's not hard to see what a child would begin to believe if a parent kept telling him or her this while growing up. While you are young, you tend to believe your parents!

I grew up with many of these feelings and ways of looking at things. I was not disappointed a lot as I brought about results that were always a result of my own thinking. My mom used to tell me not to get my hopes up, trying to protect me from the disappointments of life. Not get my hopes up?! What else is there? I had big dreams and visions of things I wanted to do, always tempered by this fact. I had thought structures that were interfering with my underlying viewpoint of what was possible. Thus, the things I was looking at were changing and flowing with what I was seeing as potential outcomes.

CHAPTER 4
THE EVOLUTION OF THOUGHT STRUCTURES: WAVES OF INFLUENCES

Influences on Thought Structures

We see increasing possibilities as the knowledge available to us expands, but there are things possible we don't even know about yet. If we acknowledge that our abilities are far beyond what we use, there are many perceptions and levels of awareness we can grow into. They will become available to us. The point is to open the door to discovering more of them, instead of simply being used to our personal status quo and looking no further. In this section we will be looking at areas of our lives where we may be "driving with the brakes on."

In general, with daily events in our lives, we just come up with ideas and what things mean on our own. Often people from the media insist on telling us what things mean when we read something, watch a TV show, or listen to a speech. Remember, thought structures are defined as ideas we build on as we go through life. We have built concepts of things that we add to as we go along. We may get lazy, though, and not really examine where that idea came from. This is where we can wind up either limiting our perspective or actually getting in own our way later on. Every now and then something may occur that goes against or completely shatters previous ideas we have held about the status quo and what can happen. When this happens, we start creating new thought structures with the new and different perspective.

For example, if a family has a house by a river that has not flooded in over 100 years and then it floods and severely damages their house, their idea of what and where is safe will become quite different. Their perspective changes. What was once perceived as safe is not considered safe anymore. Thus, different factors will most likely be included in the new evaluation of their circumstances. Certainly their thought structures about that specific event would be altered, but they might also begin to question other thought structures previously considered unshakable.

We can create these structures and then leave them there to further filter our experiences without considering them. As a result, we can create traps for ourselves that limit possibilities. These are patterns of thought, *habits* of thought. We can get so caught up in traps of our own design that we might not even look at the big picture. We can trap ourselves in small circumstances that don't matter in the grand scheme of things. Things are going on at the same time, in different dimensions and on different levels, usually unseen by us and others. Yet they are there to be seen if we are up to the task.

How many times have we criticized ourselves for a perceived mistake? Who decided it was a mistake? Why? In the bigger picture it was all experience that will be remembered by the universe and by us, as we are part of the fabric and essence of the universe. It goes on; you are magnificent and contribute to the knowledge and expansion of the universe. Everything contributes, all experiences contribute, and all experiences are valid. Nothing is wasted. It may only seem so to us at the time. Not only do we do this to ourselves, there are *influencers* everywhere in our society that "help us" decide things in unproductive ways.

When we were in the womb, we perceived our mother's emotional state, or vibration, on some level, be it happiness, fear, or anger. This provided initial cellular input and structure for our beliefs and belief systems. If she experienced fear or anger, our spiritual essence didn't agree or align with those emotions because it is not the nature of spiritual essence to harbor fear or anger. However, this provided early conflicts between our spiritual essence and the physical part of us being formed in this new life. We do wind up resonating with the vibrations going on with our mother and in the home. Our personal thought habits and ways of looking at things evolved over time, but thought structures began to form and build from these points of reference. This is part of the physical and the spiritual joining together. Physically we are vulnerable but, as spirits, we are free and unencumbered. We probably didn't go back and eliminate these early impressions of fear or anger using our spiritual essence as a model. We most likely didn't remember them!

Added on to these were the day-to-day experiences that shrink our view of the universe and all that is. Our view tends to get smaller and less broad, less focused on the universe, once becoming physical. There is no backing up or backing out of this universe unless that becomes part of our framework. Our viewpoint gets more and more oriented toward our five senses once we transition to human and spiritual from being just spiritual source. Later school comes to continue this process. We are taught to listen, focus, stop daydreaming, and to keep our feet on the ground. Bad advice, if you ask me!

Generational Consciousness Shifts as Influences on Thought Structures

As the consciousness of the world changes, generations and values change. New generations see things in different ways as their thought structures are shaped from a newer perspective. An evolution of our consciousness results.

For example, the parents of the "Baby Boomers" overcame a massive evil and conflict that threatened our world as they fought and survived World War II. But they came from a Depression-era upbringing that had values and fears learned in another time, one of incredible adversity. This in no way depreciates the value of that knowledge, but what happened as a result was a natural response, a movement closer to home. The desire to create and protect a family was strengthened and thus the "Baby Boom" generation was brought into being. Depression and World War fears were recent and powerful, and both of these monumental traumas were the hand this generation was forced to deal with. And they did. What they learned while under adverse and horrible circumstances was valuable.

I see how I was affected by the fears my mother had as a result of her earlier life circumstances. She had the fear of scarcity from growing up as a child of the Great Depression, and the fear of having a loved one off fighting a war. There is great uncertainty and vulnerability with these circumstances. I was exposed to her fears as a child, and I began designing my world with that foundation, even though those circumstances had passed. Her thought structures were part of the beginnings of mine. It is not anyone's fault; it is just an easy thing to have happen.

Every minute the world is recreating itself. It is in a constant state of flux and creation. We create it with our consciousness moment to moment. I did not realize this for a long time while growing up. I looked more at the failure that could happen, not the success that could occur. This was a thought habit my mother developed from her experience. I was building on it without being cognizant that I was doing so, just as I'm sure she had done. As a result, I withdrew from life and did not fully experience it. There was a stigma in my world about being wrong or making mistakes and being subject to ridicule that put up a whole defense shield of boredom and lack of engagement. Why try just to fail? Why appear to be stupid? The structure was totally there for this to persist. At this point in my life I experimented with drugs to see if I could still do the same things when high that I could do when not on drugs. Not being high was boring, and this was a direct result of not being willing to be fully engaged in the experience of life. It was a game of my own design that I could play, and no one would know if I was winning or losing. It was just an escape from life.

As they evolve, each generation forwards momentum and a direction in terms of progress. Thus, a change in direction for the consciousness of humanity is constantly underway. As the planet and cosmos evolve, so do we. Our awareness and knowledge increases, and what can be solved and created changes along with it.

Just like any generation the "Baby Boom" generation is part of this evolutionary change as are their children. All generations interface between what has happened in the past and the awareness shift into the future. Though every generation faces some of the same types of things, the "Baby Boom" generation began a more pronounced interfacing between the predominant force of the physicality of a world at war into the expansion of consciousness. In other words, society shifted from the harsh reality of a world at war to a world at relative peace. Families could get back to the business of living their lives and raising children instead of focusing on what was needed for the war effort. Thus, the "Baby Boomer" generation was underway and the next generational viewpoint shift had begun.

As these children grew up there was more of a reach into consciousness and what was the meaning of things. The music and culture shifted from being about "sock hops," muscle cars, and surfing to mind expansions, drug experiences, meditation, the arrival and expansion of yoga and Eastern religion, and a resulting increased focus on our "inner space."

This fact is sometimes met with sarcasm and not with the realization of evolution of the universe and that we are part of that and it is us. Older generations may not approve or understand but consciousness and knowledge push forward.

What's important consistently changes, as do values. These events of the sixties pushed a new paradigm into increased and alternative awareness.

The use of the drug LSD and its proponent, Timothy Leary, was a prime example of this. He even made the cover of *Time* magazine. Exploration and expansion of consciousness, however badly handled at the time with the use of drugs, was here to stay. With it came another shift and an influence on thought structures characteristic of each generation. Every new cutting edge is dulled by what it is cutting. That's been the history of the world. In the end, though, we are all participating knowingly or unknowingly. Each soul has a path; it is on that path, whether we are cognizant or not. The soul will wake up when it is time and when an outside force interacts with and helps it move on to the next place.

Societal Models as Influencers of Thought Structures

Events impact a society or country and we seek order. In our physical state we make use of our brains to help us handle our environment. There has been considerable research done on the uses of the left brain versus the right brain.

The left brain seeks order while the right brain provides intuitive, creative interaction with our world. It is the right brain that enables us to feel a larger sense of what is going on with us and our world. The capacity of the right brain is enormous, and it is the part that enables us to process and perceive beyond a narrow interpretation of our world.

The left brain narrows focus and has the function of providing a rational framework for information that's been learned. As something learned becomes "second nature," it has become capable of interfacing with the right intuitive processes. The capacity of the left brain is miniscule compared to the right brain.

The model currently dominant in our society, particularly in the United States, is a left-brain–ordered model. We go to school, learn, get a job, a house, work, retire, and die. Predominant influences running our society set up this order: "education" is oriented toward the left brain to serve corporate interests who need workers and people oriented toward producing and selling things. This keeps people on the path of producing and consuming, wanting, and buying. This serves those who want to expand commercial influence and accumulate money and things, but this does not particularly serve us as spirits on a journey. It does, however, allow considerable leeway to create within this model, such as creating a business. There is nothing wrong with that. Businesses produce things people need and want. They also provide innovation that enables us to do more. But they can go overboard and often do.

With our current economic system, we need to work to survive. In nature, animals must hunt in order to eat. One has always needed to produce something to exchange with others in order to survive, but our current society has moved into the era of governmental control and overregulation. We have moved further away from being self-sufficient toward being more dependent on others and on our government. This does not particularly help us as spirits. Becoming dependent can lead us to believe we have less ability and responsibility in creating our own lives. In turn, this viewpoint fosters the formation of spiritually unproductive thought structures. It causes us to unwittingly dial back our own abilities.

We have more laws, more taxes, more economic stresses, more political nonsense, constantly creating increasing headwinds. Much of our world is also set up on this model. It often takes a huge impact or event to affect consciousness on a wide scale. Often when these events are created or occur in nature we are shocked into an abrupt change in consciousness. When these events are created, they are usually in the direction that produces fear and uncertainty and consequently refocuses our attention toward ends which do not serve us on our larger paths but do serve those creating the events.

We need to stay outside this and realize *we are each on our own paths*. It is not the path of our neighbors, though it may often seem this way. Each of us has our own purpose and reason for coming back into physical form. Part of that is to help the universe continue to discover itself. We are doing the same. Death of the body is the return to our natural state, which is spirit, the non-physical. What we carry out when we leave the physical state is part of our experience database. It is ours; it is absorbed as instinct and also part of the memory of the universe. It is not lost and neither are we. Our essence remains. In a dream, we always seem to be aware of our identities. We have an awareness of who we are, even though in dreams we may not have a body or be in a situation where anything is following the rules of our physical world. It is interesting that we do always seem to know who we are in the dream. That's us, our spiritual essence and our consciousness.

Churches and Organized Religion

Churches and religious ideas have always had a considerable influence on our thought structures. Many religions and sects of major religions teach that they are the one true faith and that all others are lesser or outright wrong, that the poor souls following that faith may be lost. Numerous conflicts have been fought throughout the centuries over this underlying cause of disagreement. To me, it seems to be a complete invalidation of the concepts religions put forth. It does not seem like this could possibly be a true expression of God, yet many religious people I have talked to have this view. There is even written material that basically says following the wrong faith will result in "damnation." In the end, it serves to diminish participation by large numbers of people or attract large numbers through fear of the consequences of not believing. When I look at life and the incredible harmony that exists in nature, I can't help but acknowledge a higher consciousness that created everything in existence. I have trouble trying to assign it entity-like descriptions that many organized religions seem so intent on doing. It seems too limiting, but that is just my feeling.

I always had a difficult time with churches and organized religion, not so much for their core beliefs, but how they go about enforcing them. I know it's important to many people. Faith does have value, and I appreciate what it does for society and individuals. But, for me, it was frustrating. It is not the faith aspect but rather church protocol.

I remember sitting in the pew as a kid checking off the items in the service as we completed them. This disturbed my mother greatly. But I remember reading the prayer of confession and how the congregation would all stand up and read it together. I would not say it, though, because I did not believe that I was a sinner and not worthy to receive God, but all I had to do was "say the word and I shall be healed," or some other equivalent statement. I was just a kid, I thought, and I hadn't had time to be a sinner yet! I was not buying this prayer at all, so I would not repeat it. It just didn't add up but, looking back, this is just part of the package of formulating our viewpoints into the same framework for control to be built in. My feeling is that much of the true doctrines of the world's churches were altered long ago and corrupted for the sake of being able to exert some measure of control over parishioners. I know this viewpoint will not be popular with many, but it is what I have personally come to feel as true. There are scholars who have explored this in depth and found the same thing. (That's a thought structure I have in place!)

If we were created in God's image, and God is an infinite being with infinite capacity for love and forgiveness, infinite capacity to create and is all-knowing, then we at our spiritual essence have similar potential. We are part of God. What matters is our awareness that we possess these traits but too many material things get in the way to allow them to develop. There is too much of us wrapped into the physical character of life here in the material dimension. We could at least acknowledge that we have this capacity and become aware of things that can interfere with moving in this direction.

Detractors as Influencers of Thought Structures

There are detractors for virtually everything here on Earth. But in most cases, the universe gives us what we *expect* to happen, what we *believe* will happen. While it is true that unexpected things happen, for the most part, in our daily lives things turn out the way we think. Frank Lloyd Wright, an inspired and famous American architect, said, "The thing always happens that you really believe in, and the belief in a thing makes it happen."[1] This is true and is demonstrated over and over in our world. How many times have you seen an Olympic medalist who was interviewed and said he or she saw himself or herself there since childhood? I have seen this many times, and there are many quotes from many great people who have observed this too. William O'Neil, founder of *Investor's Business Daily*, said, "How you think is everything." This is true. But what we often miss are the habits of thought we have unconsciously developed over the years with a great deal of help from various detractors and other influences that we experience in our lives via the media, schools, or at work, just to name a few.

Detractors are generally a very miserable lot. But they are everywhere, and it is quite easy to develop thought structures or habits of thought that incorporate pieces of their viewpoints. If you are around them daily you may find yourself being careful of what you express in terms of feelings or opinions. Habitual viewpoints of how we look at things determine how we steer our lives along our paths. Being aware of these subtleties helps us to unravel the parts of our lives we do not want and create the lives we do want. But we need to realize our part in it.

Most innovative, new, or unique discoveries or perspectives that are found seem to have detractors. This is especially true with things like various new healing modalities, movies like *The Secret*, UFOs, and so forth—basically things on the cutting edge or just outside what is considered mainstream in terms of acceptance. Christopher Columbus was considered insane for not believing the Earth was flat! Louis Pasteur was considered crazy for discovering and claiming that germs were the cause of disease. There is a long list of leading-edge thinkers who were ridiculed and scorned relentlessly by such detractors. Many were even executed for having unconventional views. What if they had listened to detractors?

Having your own viewpoint is courageous; it can be extremely difficult to maintain while not succumbing to the mediocre world of the mainstream. Leading edges are always the first to experience adversity of thought, or even rough weather. We will touch on detractors in other places in this book. But new ideas that have merit and are groundbreaking readily attract detractors who will not accept them. The masses never develop new things. They often do criticize new things. There are also many who have vested interests they want to protect. There are numerous detractors of "alternative" medical and health care treatments and technology. While there are undoubtedly many people making claims that should be suspect, there are many valid therapies that may be quite effective.

Here is a story to illustrate an experience I had with a non-mainstream therapy. Toward the end of a conference I was attending, I developed a severe pain in the kidney area that then moved to the bladder. It was very intense. I got home the next day and immediately went to see my doctor, who practiced alternative therapies. His whole practice was based on this, and he was considered "nonconventional." He used a machine where I held a copper electrode in one hand

and he touched various acupressure points on my body with another electrode. He would scan for various frequencies of disease organisms, parasites, chemical pollutants, molds, and viruses, and the response was screened through a computer that would compare what he found to the frequency of that particular organism or substance. In about five minutes he found a particular strain of e-coli that he said I probably picked up from eating at a restaurant during the conference. It had gone from the kidney and lodged in the bladder. He gave me a substance to mix with water and drink that virtually latched onto the e-coli and physically dragged it out of the body via the urinary tract. Within a day, it was gone and I felt fine.

The interesting thing about this experience was that there was a medical doctor there visiting that day, observing this therapy in order to learn it and use it in his practice. He was amazed. The MD said that had I come to him, he would have ordered a series of tests and may not have found the same thing. He said they may have eventually found e-coli, but it would have taken more time and expense. According to this classically trained doctor, I most likely would have been admitted to a hospital based on my symptoms.

Later in this book we will take a look at some scientific support for the idea of our thoughts influencing outcomes. One of the researchers we will reference is Masaru Emoto. He has done some amazing work with water. He found some remarkable things with profound implications. While we are on the subject of detractors, I wanted to do a preemptive strike and mention that there are detractors to Emoto's work. They say he has not proven these things with outside observations, or that he has not done double-blind studies.

To me this just further drives home the idea of observation having affecting outcomes that we will discuss in chapter seven. If someone doubts Emoto's work, he or she obviously would not get the same results. In the strict name or discipline of science, one could say that if his results can't be duplicated by others, they must not be valid or they are at least questionable. This is an accepted condition in traditional scientific circles. However, in my opinion, this is ridiculous from a real-world, practical view. There are plenty of people who do things others can't duplicate. There are exceptional athletes, coaches, composers, artists, and business people, for example, who are talented or unique and can present ideas and do things others can't duplicate. This doesn't devalue what they do or remove it from existence. I agree there are places for strict scientific protocol, but exploring things such as Emoto has done is not one of them. His discoveries have great value as you will see.

It is very revealing that he is able to produce these effects but someone else who does not have a similar idea may not be able to. If someone doubts his work and results, it could be that they do not believe and are setting out to "prove it" while they are totally *not expecting* it will be true. What benefit is it to refute *this* particular set of observations other than to be right? I am not defending or refuting his work. I'm merely pointing out the truth behind attempts to discredit it. Often they don't serve anyone except for an ego or vested interest somewhere.

There is often an intention to discredit in an attempt to discourage the pursuit of an idea or the possibilities present if the idea were proven to be true. If there is a vested interest somewhere that will be harmed by this idea, the pressure to invalidate it is ramped up. One example of this is the invalidation of nutritional supplements by large pharmaceutical companies and the U.S. Food and Drug Administration. Prescription drugs kill tens of thousands each year, yet we sometimes see TV news shows about the dangers or ineffectiveness of nutritional supplements and herbs. What if they actually worked to keep people healthy? OH NO!! That would *not* be good for large pharmaceutical companies. I bring this up not to bash large pharmaceutical companies (well, maybe a little) but to make a point about detractors in general. Just be sure you follow your own reality and your own heart and be aware that detractors exist. Some are valid, but you should decide based on your own observations and feelings. Don't get steered off your path because of them. Many of our current problems in society have resulted from our accepting sound bites where a simple examination of facts would prove that such problems come from vested interests of some kind.

Other Factors Influencing Our World and Perceptions

Other factors exist that influence our perception and may steer our thought structures and beliefs in certain directions. Realize that we are living in an illusory world. Things are not necessarily as they seem, and much of what we "see" day to day is not as it appears to be. It is much larger than what we see; there is more going on than what we are routinely aware of, and there are things just outside of our immediate perception. We will explore the subject of integrity, which factors into this, as we go further.

Not only are our own thought structures filtering our perceptions, other factors are constantly bombarding us.

Advertising, news reports, economic statistics, government reports, politicians' accounts of things: these are all subject to interpretation and agendas. People frequently tell each other (and themselves) things that are only partly true for the purpose of maintaining an appearance of some kind. It's related to the acceptance or development of a thought structure and the maintenance of it. I bring this up because it is part of how we are steered into thinking what we think and consequently developing a picture of our world different than what it is or what could be if pure truth were utilized.

Often there are vested interests steering us into having a certain view of things. For example, sound bites are used over and over to influence us into having a certain view of things favorable to those offering them. These are frequently used in politics, advertising, and education. We just need to be aware of how often these types of things occur and that they can shape our opinions in ways not necessarily supported by data. Finding things out for ourselves is the best way to reach an opinion about something. But, if the use of such techniques effectively *steer* us in a certain direction, we may develop opinions and their associated thought structures without realizing how we came to those beliefs. This then causes us to automatically reject opposing or different viewpoints.

Ideas float around the universe. They may or may not be yours. But, since we are connected to everything, we have the capability of perceiving them. There are millions of ideas and thoughts. Often we perceive them without necessarily being aware they are there or have just arrived. These ideas may or not be directed toward you. You could just be in the area they are in or be in the flow of ideas and thoughts as they pass through. For example, if you are in a crowd you may get ideas or thoughts that are not normally what you might think of. Thoughts can come from other beings. Just because you perceive them does not mean they came from you. It is important to know this and not cultivate or let undesirable ideas and thoughts hang around. Many people do this unknowingly or unintentionally and can begin to feel there is something wrong with them as a result of having these thoughts. Sometimes just being in a space with a wide variety of people is enough to pick up thoughts that might be unsettling or unnerving. I notice this in large crowds. It is the overall energy of the crowd that can bring this about. I am aware of that and don't take on things that aren't mine. If I don't want to entertain those thoughts, I focus on something else.

Noticing Our Thought Structures

It is easy to build on thoughts by wondering where they came from and why you thought them. We have threads of thoughts. We will think of something. One thought will lead to another and another, until we wonder how we got on that subject. Have you ever noticed yourself dwelling on some thought and wondering how you got there? Maybe you were talking with someone, you were having a conversation and somehow you got onto a train of thought totally different than what you had been on. You may have wondered how you arrived at such a thought. Thoughts are often connected in seemingly unrelated ways, but your mind will connect them via some memory or trace of some other time. At this point is it easy to negatively attribute this to being scattered, but that is not necessarily so. It is easy to add onto thought structures when this happens. During the numerous times this has happened, some piece of data landed and piled onto an existing thought structure somewhere, often without our awareness. Our minds are amazing; the right brain can literally connect billions of pieces of information. Knowing this will help you see and disassemble unproductive thought structures as you move forward.

Realize the mind is working all the time and is frequently on "autopilot." When this occurs, notice it and have fun tracing the chain of connected thoughts that got you on the new subject. This is how the mind works; realize that without being aware of this activity, you can find yourself building patterns and habits of thought. All this might not even be coming from you. You can learn to control and redirect your thoughts. *You* are not your mind. Learn to direct unwanted thoughts away from you. Just turn them off and focus on something else. Sometimes it works best to just quiet your mind from everything for a short while with some breathing. You won't be able to stop thoughts from coming in but, when the unwanted thoughts occur, just dismiss them and re-quiet your mind. Realize that allowing stray thoughts to hang around that may not even be yours is one way negative patterns can develop. By unknowingly entertaining them you can wind up building upon them and creating things for yourself that you do not want. And they were not even yours to begin with!

Thoughts can also be implanted. Media, advertising, microwaves, subliminal messages, and thoughts from others are all flowing around us all the time. These can be perceived by us on some level because we have the sense and perceptual ability to do so. But we have not really acknowledged it or allowed it to develop.

There is a more sinister side to this, too. The pharmaceutical industry advertises heavily and suggests medication that places our attention on these conditions and gets us to wonder about them. These companies do also produce many valuable products to be fair to them. Just remember, attention on something is the first step in bringing about its manifestation. While it doesn't happen right away, developing a thought structure and habitually thinking about something will eventually bring it about.

Why is bad or alarming news repeated over and over? Who got the idea that this is the only model for news programs? Look at the news media and television in general. This is a good example of how thoughts are implanted or transmitted to us that we can adopt as a viewpoint and begin building onto our existing thought structures without paying much attention to it. When hearing young children recite advertising phrases they see and hear on TV, we realize how much sources that are not of their own origin or discovery shape their world. Their thought structures are being constantly influenced by this. Combine this with the other noise in their worlds and one can see how pervasive this is, how it can shape things in a way that can lead them off their paths and purposes.

Take for example the idea of broadcasting things with the tools we have and we can see how many things just get picked up by cultures or people in cities. Subliminal messages in advertisements were outlawed long ago but there are still subliminal messages in TV programming. This often comes in the form of insinuation. Broadcasting these messages into the airwaves can result in attitudes being picked up and stored. Here is another point to consider that is not specifically related to messages being broadcast. It is the amount of electronic "noise" that is generated from the vast number of electronic devices and electromagnetic frequencies being used for cell phones and microwaves. Because of this, it is no wonder that there is more confusion in thought and our attention spans have become so short. The amount of data streaming around the world now is staggering compared to what was happening merely twenty-five years ago. That is a very short time compared to age of the universe and even relatively short when looking at our current life expectancy.

There is evidence to show that electromagnetic frequencies (EMFs)and data flows are having an effect on our perception and our health. I mention this merely to increase the awareness of how our paths can become altered by inadvertent and unconscious reception of ideas that are not of our own creation. Being aware of this helps us become less worried about ourselves if we have seemingly unusual ideas. They may not have originated within us. How many kids as young as two or three years old recite advertising jingles? Most of us can also remember many of these from our childhood. The repetition of these influences our choices in many cases. Most of the time this is not particularly destructive but it is used here as an example of the power of repetition of an idea.

It's getting increasingly difficult to find a place on Earth free from EMFs. These alter and mostly interfere with perception. After all, the body is a biological organism and functions with electrical energy as a normal part of cellular and brain function. Microwave electrical energy from cell phones, cell towers, and TETRA masts can interfere with biological function as well as thought function. Here is quote from British author and researcher David Icke:

> TETRA-type technology operates at a pulsing frequency in the range of 17.6 Hz. This is close to the wavelengths of brain activity and so it interferes with the electrical (and therefore every other) system of the brain. This accounts not only for physical and immune system effects, as the communication from brain to body is short circuited, it also explains mental and emotional consequences like depression and inability to concentrate.[2]

These can have a long-term effect on the thought structures we are operating with and creating. Knowing this and knowing yourself can keep these effects to a minimum. You can learn to recognize when you are being influenced and not just begin to think you are losing your mind. There's no need to fear these energies. The awareness that they exist can diffuse the effect on us quite efficiently.

Steering Yourself and Getting Control

Learning to understand ourselves better and knowing this information helps us become aware of thought structures and how they come to be. This is a preemptive strike against creating unwanted thought structures and then acting on these thought structures unconsciously. It is not necessary to go back and trace all these unwanted thought structures back to their origin. The numbers of incidents and thoughts in your total existence is far too vast to make that even possible, and it is not necessary.

Be aware of your current thought environment and what you want for your life. Don't take on things just because they occurred to you. *Stay focused on the thoughts that are constructive to you, helping you expand your awareness, and helping you create the life you want to create.* I've taken on many thoughts inadvertently. Then I wonder why I have them, where I got them, and how this could change everything. This is not constructive. It is distracting and no doubt has caused many people to question their sanity and seek help. It helps to be aware that there are ideas and thoughts out there that are purposely sent and imbued with a lower vibration knowing people will entertain them and thus keep them in a state of fear, with doubts and wonderings. Fear sells. Knowing this can help you avoid taking on destructive ideas just because they are out there.

Just remember that everything that exists was a thought first. By continually thinking something is a certain way, the "self-fulfilling prophecy" takes place. This is the Law of Attraction at work. This law has Biblical roots. In their book, *Ask and It Is Given,* Esther and Jerry Hicks define the Law of Attraction: "things of like vibration are drawn together."[3] Here is another excellent explanation:

> The basic definition of Law of Attraction states that energy attracts to itself other energy with which it's in vibrational resonance with. Both the nonphysical and physical aspects of our Universe are made up of energy and intelligence that vibrates. Nothing rests. The difference between the physical and the nonphysical is the rate of vibration.[4]

This is the way things come into being in this physical plane of existence. Thus, we can understand that thoughts eventually turn into things with continued attention and contributing action. Being aware of this also explains how so many things come into existence that we may not want. If you were trying to create or change a world, you could do it simply by steering people into thinking thoughts of a certain vibration on a continuous basis. Tuning forks begin to vibrate when near a vibrating tuning fork that is of the same frequency. People can do the same. Organizations could do this to meet their goals if they were so inclined. We see this all the time in politics. It is possible that people can change their vibrations and begin resonating with those vibrations after hearing the same message over and over. If they begin to agree with it, then they can begin resonating with that idea.

Quieting the Mind

It is valuable to practice quieting the mind and be still for a while. If you're not used to this practice, you may feel a bit uneasy or uncomfortable. When I initially began learning and practicing this, I felt like I had to do, see, or hear something. I was used to lots going on all at once at a rapid pace.

I worked as a securities trader many years ago. While sitting at the trading desk, there was a constant stream of activity and information flow. I was watching six computer screens, calling in orders, and listening to orders being reported back. You get used to that. Purposefully shutting it off for a while takes practice.

One of my favorite places to go is the mountains. If there is no wind or no birds singing, there is absolutely no sound, except for a slight hum of the energy of Earth. For me, experiencing this is a joy and a peaceful experience. You can actually have your perception available to experience new things instead of a constant barrage of noise, media, phones, and conversations. Initially the quiet made me uneasy. Gradually I have changed my lifestyle. For me this is now more normal, and it enables me to be more in the moment, more able to visualize what I want to create, and enjoy moving toward it.

Thought energy is the beginning of building something. It is the prototype, so to speak, that first takes place in the mind. Continuing focus brings it more and more into the physical world. It's continuing a thought structure. At their foundation, all things are energy, so putting thought focus on something is the very beginning of its formation.

Remember the analogy of a thought structure as a building on a foundation. This foundation was something first; an idea that then became a belief. Then other ideas latched onto it, thereby building the thought structure. It then may wind up being defended and solidified. Sometimes we are aware of what we were putting there, but other times things have been built without us paying attention to what was happening.

On most levels our society encourages demonstrating ego-based superiority. To a large extent much of our world is set up around this concept. Because our society pushes things that promote the ego, it can devalue self-esteem and add to a person's negative perception of themselves. This is a problem. As I went through the different phases of my life and my discoveries, I found myself in careers that followed this line of thinking. The left brain, the logical part of the mind, was so involved in the day-to-day activities that I tended to lose myself and get less creative. I can see how this created problems for me in the past.

Creativity is housed in the right brain. Usually by just getting away from the problem, I've had solutions come to me in ways I never would have thought of by sitting at my desk "working on the problem." It can often be totally different than the line of thought I was looking at before. This can be explained by the following. Jerry and Esther Hicks have been speaking and writing about insights received from a group of non-physical beings and advisors known to them collectively as "Abraham." Jerry and Esther have released many books and CDs featuring the wisdom of Abraham, about the Law of Attraction and how it works in our lives. I refer to several quotes from Abraham in places throughout this book. I have found the Hicks' work with Abraham to be very helpful and insightful in becoming more aware of how we construct our lives and vibrations. Abraham reminds us that problems and solutions are on different vibrational levels.

I used to wake up in the morning worried, having been mentally "working on something" as I was in the process of waking up. I was evaluating my performance against some ego-based standard, and then being critical of my progress. When I got up, it subsided. But, if that vibration was active within me, I would take it too seriously and then wonder why or if I was defective. What's important is remembering we are on our own paths. What matters is how we are dealing with this type of experience and reconciling it in our own minds. What's not productive is the tendency to compare ourselves to others. Our world is so geared toward this that it is very difficult not to do. It is especially difficult with any type of economic, legal, or medical stresses added. But having the awareness about ourselves and where we are on our journey will make this easier to handle.

Often there's little or no acknowledgement of creativity within a day's activities. There might be time set aside for this but it is considered outside the core activities and, in many cases, it is being phased out of the schools.

According to Albert Einstein, creativity or imagination is more important than intelligence, though both are obviously necessary. I consider this when observing the universe, and having thought frameworks in place can actually limit perception of what is possible. We can see this if we consider the creativity in dreams and how they seem to make sense when we are asleep, then seem incongruous with reality when we wake up and try to explain them. In dreams we are in another dimension, so things work there that don't work in this dimension. Your identity is pretty much always intact, even in dreams, as I mentioned earlier. Dreams can teach us about creativity and are in large part the right brain tying things together that have been active in our recent activity or attention.

Trying to fit the dream world into the rules of this universe does not work. As Dr. Richard Bartlett, author of *Matrix Energetics* (Atria, 2009), has said, "You can't observe something breaking the rules using the rules you're observing it with."[5] Naturally we just select this universe as the one that takes priority over the dream world. This is starting to change a bit because more and more people are simply refusing to get shoved into molds of the past. They see that maybe it has not worked and this is why they are changing their view. But we must be cognizant of pushing ourselves back into our own molds and thought structures. These are just patterns and habits of thought and must be broken to make changes in our lives. Dr. Bartlett also notes, "As long as we are dissatisfied with the way things are, without changing the way we observe them, we continue them."[6]

It's easy to negatively or positively evaluate and compare ourselves to others, to what we see advertised and things all around us. We are told what the standards are, and we don't necessarily re-evaluate them for what they are: someone's opinion and idea of what should be that has taken hold and defined our world. There are increasing numbers of people who don't accept this pattern. The universe is taking hold of some things and reality is shifting. Awareness is expanding. We are realizing the limited workability of our current model.

Each generation is faced with new challenges. Each generation gets to set the world onto another course. It is always a struggle because people comfortable with the old model resist change to a large degree. The new will always be difficult for many. Yet this is the evolution of the universe, and every generation experiences this.

CHAPTER 5
BREAKING OUT OF PATTERNS

Examples of Patterns of Thought and an Outcome

Looking back at my life, I've observed thought patterns that contributed to my being stuck or unenthusiastic about life. There have been times when I've been uncomfortable with myself, not living in the moment, or not noticing that I had conflicts. As a result, I wasn't sorting them out. While this was going on, I experienced discouragement and the feeling of no real goals and progress in life—nothing new or exciting. That was the result of that mindset. In this condition, the left brain frets, worries, and tries to solve this without looking at the whole underlying thought structure.

I had always been restless and spent much of my life seeking sensation and activities of my own choosing, not any real career for long periods. I was resisting the system we have that often forces us to do things unrelated to our interests and desire for happiness. It is an unfulfilled life under these circumstances, and it is easy to keep it in place in our society. In this condition, it is easy to keep non-optimum thought foundations in place and build upon them. You'll have lots of company.

The following is an example of a thought structure and behavior pattern I had in place years ago and how it was running along and filtering my thoughts and dictating my responses to events and circumstances. I began realizing that I had spent a great deal of my life looking for a career that would be interesting enough to be passionate about. My lack of interest manifested itself in my not fully participating or experiencing things related to work. I was pretty much bored with everything, so I didn't want to get too involved—it was more of an annoyance than anything else. To some degree I believe I was also trying to fulfill someone else's expectations that I would have a career that was prestigious, something I (or, rather, they) could be proud of. This was all part of the ego-based structure I had grown up with and that had been reinforced by the society around me. But I had put it there as a structure and was holding it in place without seeing it.

As a result of this thought structure and resulting behavior, I was holding myself back and not really experiencing things. I was also assembling lists of accomplishments that I thought would impress those around me. I was searching for what interested me, but I was not really finding anything that fit. I was also looking at things that were thought of as good criteria for what to pursue, using that as a filter. I was not living in my heart, but instead in my mind and ego. This is one reason why my interest level was so low.

Most of these activities turned out to be short-term careers. I was *almost* getting involved in things, hoping to become interested. I was not being honest with myself in these circumstances because I was doing things for the purpose of saying I had done them or for money, not because I was necessarily happy doing them. Once I saw this, it was easier to be honest with myself and not worry about the ego-based perceptions of a career. There are so many ways to look at things. I had been filtering these things, using a thought structure of my own creation.

Having what turns out to be short-term careers may be necessary to discover what you're *not* interested in. Usually it is a stepping stone and a useful gathering of knowledge on the way to finding something you *are* interested in. *No experience is wasted!* Along the way there were also things I happily poured my heart and soul into. Nowadays this is how I tell if it's worthwhile and on the path I had planned when arriving here in this lifetime. I will feel it is right, but this has taken practice and maturity. I had to stop filtering things through someone else's criteria that I had adopted as my own. I had to discover I was doing this and start being honest with myself.

The bright side is I have gained knowledge and much experience by finding things I was not ultimately interested in. And who is to say we need to do the same thing our whole lives anyway? The financial rewards can be good for doing that, and we certainly generate points of stability that way in terms of our current society, but I'm not sure about the evolution of our consciousness when we are doing that. This is also how we get trapped in a rut. We are fluid beings, and we should make sure we are staying where we are because we love what we are doing—not because we are afraid to try something else. I know that's easy for me to say. But, again, this gets back to integrity to one's self, being honest with one's self and not remaining trapped because we feel we can't get out. If you are trapped, start creating a plan to extricate yourself by creating a new story. Let the universe help you find your next direction.

Being in the Moment

It is beneficial to be fully willing and available to experience, and is something I am continually seeking to improve. After all, the universe is being created one moment at a time, and it is up to us to realize it and create from that aspect. Recognize when something takes you out of the moment. Many things can do this.

For example, the media seems merely to remind us of what has happened (over and over again). This is creating a vibration, a wavelength of thought in each of us. How we react to it, and how often we repeat it—thus creating more similar thoughts—adds to our thought structures and makes it more likely that they will endure. Don't dwell on things except what you want to create. Visualizing how you want things to be is time well spent, but dwelling on past misfortunes or disagreements and playing them out over and over simply continues negative patterns. It is best to work on staying in the moment.

There are many people walking around in a trance who are told what to think and they are not questioning it. The structure of our economic system makes this more likely. It installs thought structures. Actually it is the individual who does it, but there are indoctrinating things, such as political sound bites, advertising, or things our parents or friends repeat, everywhere that steer and encourage us to be this way. Once the foundations of these ideas are in place, building on them is easy, if we are unaware. A person who is looking at something a certain way will see through that filter and continue to build upon that viewpoint.

Underlying Influences on Thought Structures

So much of our time is taken up with making a living. Between taxes and overall costs of living, many people have had to resort to the two-salary family; in generations before, one was fine. This has caused other problems besides financial ones, but underneath this is the view of what constitutes a good life in our eyes and the eyes of our society. Things are changing and that's a good thing. Of course, things are always changing, but the direction and magnitude of the change may not have been as apparent as it is now. People want more integrity, and breakdowns in integrity are very visible in this world of bloggers and 24/7 international news.

This is being brought more to light as people are demanding more truth and less spin. This is part of the universe cycle we are in now. Almost everyone I talk to feels the shift of time and energy and how it is impacting them, even very young people. I believe we are waking up. It is my opinion that often the news media is being used to paint a picture that steers us into making decisions and adding to our thought structures, keep us in certain vibrational patterns.

But there has *never* been more truth available. The Internet has made more information accessible than ever before. And even though there is also a great deal of misinformation, governments and vested interests no longer have a monopoly over what information flows out. The blogosphere has enabled a high number of astute and informed people to publish what they see, and much of this information would never find its way onto a mainstream TV station or a newspaper. This is a good thing, as the mainstream media and politicians merely push the agenda of those seeking to shape public opinion. Most of the major media outlets are owned by only six corporations. This means that messages that get repeated and appear so widespread and coming from everywhere are really coming from the same small group of media companies.

The Internet has already produced quite a lot of change in people's perception. As a result more people are engaged in what's going on. This is a good thing for our world.

Subtle Beliefs and Conflicts

Getting back to the subject of conflicts and inner conflicts, understand they can be quite subtle and therefore difficult to detect. If you look at an object in the room, you would not see atoms with electrons whizzing around. But that is the essence of what is occurring. Similarly, conflicts and beliefs can go unnoticed just because we get used to them. This can result in periods where nothing in your life seems like it is progressing. It could be a problem that isn't resolving despite your best intentions and efforts. I have found this to be the case when looking at areas of my life that weren't going well.

This can be particularly pervasive in the areas of our lives where there is a lot of emotional involvement. Usually there will be beliefs that conflict with goals. One example of this is finance. In fact, there are a whole series of agreed-upon statements in the areas of investing and finance that are conflicting and can be adopted as beliefs. They can render us stuck and ineffective when dealing with this subject. Beliefs can become installed without us realizing they have become part of how we view our world.

Here is an example of one such time when I was building some very negative thought structures. I sat next to a guy who had the most negative view of the world I have ever seen. He had totally negative views of everything and this began wearing off on me. When I realized this (quite some time later), I resigned and decided to go my own way. He was a very bright guy and was right on many issues, but this was an example of an interpretation of life and how one looks at things. He would only read information that coincided with his view; everything else was totally wrong. There was virtually nothing that he was positive on. Everybody was lying; everything was rigged, on and on.

I left there drained every night. It's not productive or healthy to remain in the company of those with such powerful negative vibrations, even though you can love them and respect them and appreciate their viewpoints—I did. It is probably harmful for you to stay, so consider that. Think of the thoughts you are attracting and installing into your mental database. I find myself spotting some of these attitudes affecting my performance to this day as a result of this time spent there. There are pieces of conflicting data and beliefs that have stuck and I am peeling them off as I find them. I was aware of many of them at the time, but the number of related ideas I continue to find is dramatic.

This building of belief systems is commonly quite automatic and it evolves into thought structures. It is through these that we filter information and determine what it means to us. It's easy to miss that it's happening. It is how we drift off course.

Another example is when we get feedback or input from our friends we admire and respect. They tell us something we ought to be doing or not doing (peer pressure). The self-evaluation process can start and may wind up with a decision on our part. This particularly happens when we're young because we're looking for points and facts to use as our "software program" for dealing with life. This influences our career decisions and much more. It can get quite pervasive and subtle. We only need to become aware of it so we are not unconsciously adding to it day by day. Just walk around and listen to conversations. You'll hear people telling you things all the time that are examples of the belief systems *they* have, and they are there because *they* have put them there by deciding they are true. It gets back to the cycle of observing something, making a decision on it, and then going with it as if it were a fact of the universe—and not just a fact they have decided on that the universe is making true *because they decided it*. Being aware of this enables us to catch ourselves in this procedure. Impressions received can get added to belief systems, and this process just continues throughout life unless we spot it and begin reversing it.

Society also "helps" us with this. Politics has become a good example. Politics has increasingly become overrun with sound bites and constant campaigning. Party positions are stated over and over until we believe that one party stands for one set of ideals and another party stands for something different. Sound bites on the news, headlines, and accounts of things that have a political agenda behind them get repeated over and over. Most people are too busy with their daily routines to invest time sorting out facts and determining the accuracy of these sound bites. And often they are just not that interested. There is a huge amount of contradictory information given out and repeated, so there's no way to sort out what it all means without a considerable investment of time.

Thus, we get impressions all day long on TV, radio, and the Internet that are in fact steering us into believing things are a certain way. For the most part, general populations have trusted their public officials to make rational decisions and trusted the media to be mostly honest and objective. In the past few years, we've seen how big a mistake this was. People who are trying to create certain states of existence, such as global governance, are busy using this factor. They are working to create impressions because they know people act on what they believe and what they believe can be steered in subtle ways. "A belief is just a thought you keep thinking…"[1] says Abraham. This can be anything that is repeated enough that you come to accept it as truth.

Conflicts come from thought structures that are not in alignment or are directly opposed. This is the basis of non-optimum performance; I have seen this in myself. It is just a matter of deciding to deal with and make a decision on these points after discovering they are not in harmony. Many times I have not done this. That is why I have not gotten better results in the past. However, seeing it is the first step in dealing with it. Then look at the explanation you give yourself. What's your account of what is happening? This is the concept of the story you are telling yourself and others about your life. Are you telling yourself you are worthy? You really are.

Dissolving Problems

Often society makes it difficult to be fluid. This is by design. There is a penalty for getting behind on bills or other problems, and the social stigma can be great. Many of us have experienced this at some point in our lives, and it can continue to have influence. I recognized this and have stopped letting it trap me like it has many times earlier in my life. We wind up essentially working for credit card companies, car loan companies, and mortgage companies (banks mostly). Most people pay their bills to these companies before they pay themselves and wind up not being financially secure as a result.

It is a well-established statistic that 95 percent of people that reach the age of sixty-five are not financially able to be self-sufficient without working. That means the banks, credit card, and finance companies have a pretty good system for trapping people and the expectations of our society greatly contribute to pushing us into this trap. There is a penalty for not paying others, but the penalty for not paying ourselves, though not as urgent, is much greater, because it's longer term. This is another "steering influence" on our lives.

As a related note, there are some great programs for helping you get out of debt and become financially more viable. These are tools you can use to help create a new story and have it be believable, because you have an effective methodology to make your vision real and workable. When you have something tangible that will help you overcome a real barrier, the new vision can become more believable, and you can then expect it to happen the way you want.

The "Debt-Free and Prosperous Living" Basic Course is an excellent program by John Cummuta. You can get information on this on Google or Amazon.com. Another person helping with this is Dave Ramsey who has a TV show and books that provide excellent advice on the concept of debt reduction. This is one example of how we can solve a problem that we have allowed to determine and shape our paths. Find some information that can help you turn around your beliefs, even if it is a little at a time. Having a viable plan that helps us change a problem area can also help us gradually reshape our beliefs and thought structures in a particular area. Having some success at turning around a problem makes it easier to further change our beliefs and begin to trust the outcome will be what we want.

I stuck with a financial theme in this short section (and in others), but it can apply to other areas as well. There are always solutions for dissolving problems, and it begins with thought structures (of course). Know there are solutions. By knowing this you will be more likely to find something that will work well. Then this helps change your beliefs. They get stronger and then you attract more of what you want. The cycle repeats. Remember how the universe works if we let it. Whether it's in the area of finance, relationships, or whatever, know and believe things will continue to realign for you.

Restoring Integrity and Trust

People want integrity and the demand for it is strengthening now more than ever. That is part of the current awakening of our consciousness in this age. Most people want integrity. Failing to deliver integrity and truth is the root cause of most of the problems we find ourselves in, both individually and as a society. By providing truth we provide clarity and allow a greater level of growth. It has become a continuing feature of our society to basically lie about things, but that's beginning to change. Of course, it still occurs, but an increasing number of people are becoming intolerant of untruths. Lack of truth eventually blows up and becomes a much bigger problem.

Politics is a great example of this. Lies fall on top of other lies until the picture is so altered it bears no similarity to actual events and sets of lies are being argued about. The truth is on an entirely different level. All this for the sake of pursuing goals that have only temporary gain involved and the gain itself is of little value. Lack of integrity seems more obvious than ever before. This is because of the stark contrast between the demand for it and the obvious lack of it in current events.

Another good example of this is in the financial markets. Companies report earnings, organizations report statistics, but those reports are frequently altered or spun to create an impression that is not the simple truth. They have been filtered through "permissible" parameters or laws of accounting. These can be arbitrary or ambiguous in places and allow some leeway.

There needs to be flexibility, but intentional lack of integrity just creates a certain impression that is untruthful. Investors want to be able to determine where investing will enable them to increase the money they earn. People planning things just need the truth. Those who lack integrity play games and create mistrust. This is still part of our evolution, but more and more people are realizing it is a destructive part of our world. This creates cynicism on the part of the public and causes disillusionment.

Wall Street and politicians are famous for this. It has come to be expected, and that is sad. It has to change. Trust and respect have to be earned. When it is repeatedly demonstrated that we cannot trust someone or some institution, it eventually becomes the subject of ridicule and is shunned until it changes and establishes a long enough track record to change the public perception. To restore any level of trust can take a very long time, perhaps generations. We can probably all think of some occasion where our trust was betrayed by someone we knew, or by a politician, friend, or business partner. That's one reason as we get older we can become so cynical and wary. We can set up thought structures around such events and people. Be aware of this!

CHAPTER 6
THE POWER OF BELIEFS:
THE POWER WE HAVE OVER OURSELVES

Examples of Beliefs

I am going to use the area of finance again to show some examples of conflicting ideas because it is a subject commonly at the center of attention in many situations and affects large numbers of people. The amount of conflicting data in this subject is vast, and the average person winds up doing nothing or very little because of this. Consequently, dealing with this area frequently gets put off for long periods of time.

There are beliefs in all areas and subjects. Here are some common examples of ideas and beliefs frequently called "conventional wisdom" in the area of finance and the markets:

- Real estate always appreciates in value.
- The stock market always goes up over time, so you

should have a long-term time horizon for investing.

- The economy is doing poorly; the stock market must also do poorly.
- Always stay invested in the market, continue putting money in regardless of what it is doing.
- The experts always know better than I do, so I should listen to them.

Though these are just examples in one area, other frequently repeated beliefs can exist in any area of life. We have been conditioned to believe many of these ideas by those selling stocks or real estate. If you study the stock or real estate markets to any great degree, you will find plenty of conflicting information, much of it that conflicts with the above ideas or beliefs. When this happens you may have difficulty implementing a plan that goes against beliefs you have adopted.

Dr. David Hawkins, author of *Power vs. Force* (Hay House, 2010), said this in a lecture I attended: "Belief systems overrule the rational mind." The thing is *we create our beliefs* either consciously or unconsciously. Remember, "A belief is just a thought you keep thinking." It is something you have come to resonate with. We would be well served to ask where that belief came from. Did we create it or was it given to us, accepting it without thinking about it? When a long-held belief is shown to be wrong, it can be either unsettling or a joyous experience. Either way it is a shift. You can create that shift by changing the way you look at things.

I have had experience with this and see these conflicts because I worked in the financial markets for a long time. For example, buying real estate with zero money down was recommended, while at the same time someone else might have the viewpoint that this is a bad idea. There are conflicting ideas constantly coming to light. Without being able to trust your own viewpoint and see your own conflicting beliefs, you'll be hesitant and do nothing (which yet another talking head will say is bad).

It is important to recognize the difference between an idea and a belief. You may hear an idea that sounds like it has merit, but hesitation may mean there is a conflicting belief underlying the confidence to act. It could be something like, "I don't trust these guys; I did something like that before and it did not work for me. Things like this don't generally turn out like they say." Be honest with yourself; you may hear or see something that sounds good, *but what do you really believe will happen with you?* This answer comes from within.

I mentioned this quote from Abraham earlier. Here is more of that quote. "A belief is only a thought you continue to think. A belief is a vibration that you have practiced often enough that now it is dominant and therefore comes up easily and often. A belief is a vibrational point of attraction that brings evidence of itself to you."[1]

Revisiting the area of finance once again, here is a personal example from my experience with trading and investing. I would not completely follow instructions for a trading system because I didn't believe it would work after doing some testing on it. So I became skeptical and wouldn't do that system because my belief was that it wouldn't work as represented. I have seen this time and time again. This is why I developed a belief and expectation. What I *expected* is what would most likely happen. It was the thought I kept thinking. It was my thought structure.

Remember the observation of Frank Lloyd Wright: "The thing always happens that you really believe in, and the belief in a thing makes it happen." If this is negative, you need to be able to change it; you can do this little by little if it seems too big to change all at once. You can do this by changing the habitual way you look at it.

Regarding beliefs as they relate specifically to stock trading (but really applicable to any belief), a well-known trading coach and psychologist, Van K. Tharp, says this about a specific belief: "Get the idea to take responsibility for it. It's giving you the result you actually expect." By exploring this as a thought structure, you can go about dismantling it and reconstructing it to serve you in the way you want it to. A belief is just part of a thought structure. A thought structure is more elaborate as the result of associated beliefs and all the other accompanying considerations that have been built around these beliefs. By changing some of the more outlying beliefs, you can begin to change the underlying belief. As Dr. Wayne Dyer said in a televised lecture I was watching, "When you change the way you look at things, the things you look at change." This is totally true. We will touch upon this again soon. If you have beliefs that are opposing each other, the result is usually no progress—or negative progress—in that area. It is also possible you don't realize they are there opposing each other.

Here's an exercise to try: (Keep this very simple.)

- Find an area that you have been working on for a time with no real progress. Look and see if there are some underlying beliefs conflicting with what you are trying to accomplish in that area. What instantly comes to mind is probably the most accurate.

- List out any steps you have taken to resolve those issues.
- Look for ideas or beliefs you have that conflict with the steps that were supposed to resolve these issues.
- See what part you played in creating the circumstance where the belief won. Realize that what you *believe* and *expect* will make it happen. *Be glad it works this way because that means you can undo it!*
- Find some points you can see that can be changed, and began looking at it differently. This can be a little at a time. Look at what you can do to change the outcome.

Be honest with yourself on what has taken place, the response you have given, and what the real motives were behind it. You don't have to tell anyone; this is just for you. I used to get mad and lie to myself sometimes, trying to convince myself of something. The thing is *I always knew*. It is okay to be honest with yourself. You don't have to explain it to anyone else unless you want to. Forgive yourself if you need to. Always forgive yourself. Learn to trust yourself. At your essence you are brilliant. If you have thoughts that immediately come up and refute this, there are most likely beliefs there that are holding you back. It's like driving with the brakes on. Here are a few more things to do.

- Take a few moments every day and focus on times you did something really right.
- Then imagine more of these times.
- When you are ready for bed at end of the day, look at the things you did right, not all the things you didn't get done.

I used to have a habit of focusing on all the things that I didn't get done during a day. I began undoing that thought habit. I would catch myself when doing it and just stop and look at what I *did* get done; I focused on the positive aspects of my life.

Here's an example of the above exercise. A friend of mine, Michael, was having trouble spending less than he made. This problem had been going on for years, and he had not made any real progress on it. He had a decent amount of money set aside from a previous circumstance, but had trouble with cash flow. He was living off his savings. He had the potential of making money off of investments and that was his plan. But he never consistently pulled it off.

He had taken several steps to resolve this. First he cut back on expenses and controlled his spending better. This helped but the underlying problem remained. He had spent money on investment programs and training in how to use the market to make more money but did not put any of it to use.

We then took a look at why he was not using what he had learned. We also discovered he had enough to make a positive cash flow. He found the underlying belief that he was mistrustful of the markets and therefore skeptical of most of the methods that he had studied to improve his investment results. His belief was that the financial markets were always on the verge of crashing, so he was afraid to participate to the degree necessary to bridge the gap between his spending and his income. Once he saw this belief, it became possible for him not only to create a plan to participate, but also a plan to exit in the event of an adverse market event. We worked out what criteria he would use for this, and he began to fare much better. He could see what ideas he had held onto that prevented implementation of his plan. Now he is moving forward with success. The other thing he started doing was looking at the times he had really been successful. He imagined more of those and his overall average vibration began rising. He was seeing more success so it became easier to visualize more. This became an upward spiral.

SECTION 3:

THOUGHT ENERGY AND TRANSMISSION

CHAPTER 7
HOW ALL THIS WORKS

Observation as a Force

In this section we will examine a number of scientifically based factors that show what happens when we decide something, and the action that happens on a cellular level. These facts support the idea of realities resulting from our thoughts. There really is a great deal of evidence for this and it is very interesting. Remember the statement from Dr. Wayne Dyer's televised lecture: "When we change the way we look at things, the things we look at change." This is true in so many ways. We know that if we look at some event as an opportunity, rather than misfortune, our outlook changes. But there is even more to this statement, as we shall see.

Science has discovered that the very act of observing something can change the thing being observed.[1] This is huge in its implications. The actual energy of attention can change things. Someone not believing something may see a different result. This has been the case with Masaru Emoto and his experiments with water crystals mentioned earlier. Detractors of something who have the energy and intention of detracting or disproving something will most likely produce a different result when doing experiments or research. The gardener with a green thumb, and love for the act of caring for plants and a garden, will produce a different outcome than someone who is indifferent to plants despite following the same regimen.

Here's an example of how caring for something can have an effect on outcomes. I know a woman who raised goats and loved doing so. She loved her animals. She and her husband got divorced, and initially she moved to a place where she had no room for her goats. Her ex-husband continued to care for them. He did not like them, however—and despite following her instructions in caring for them—they produced little or no milk. When she got a place where she could keep the goats she brought them there, and they began producing at a high volume again. Everything alive responds to love. Even machines respond to harmony.

But to some degree, things also respond simply to the act of observing, the energy of attention. Here is a quote from *Matrix Energetics*:

> Current science accepts that the act of observing something, at least at the subatomic level, changes the behavior and characteristics of the thing observed. This implies that consciousness has a direct and observable effect on the structure or composition of matter. This has been borne out in so many classic experiments in quantum physics that it is now considered a fundamental principle.[2]

Looking at other people in a certain way can cause them to change their thoughts or feelings when they see you. Though this change can be as a result of your expression, it is an energy flow of sorts and can change the person receiving the "look." Intention can be communicated, and it can be done even without a particular expression. There is a connection that is perceived. But merely the act of focusing on something directs some form of energy toward that thing. This can and apparently does affect the energy at the quantum level.

Quantum physics is finding out things that cannot be explained using previous scientific boundaries. But this is growth and the evolution of knowledge; it is of us. There is a great deal of research on this, and it is fascinating. The boundaries of what is accepted and considered to be "real" are expanding and changing rapidly.

We filter and interpret from our own thought structures and those we unknowingly absorbed as we were growing up. Yet all of us are similar: we are souls on a path that have returned to the physical. It makes sense to help each other or at least see each other as who we are in basic form, in *spirit* form. This can be difficult with many people we encounter, but seeing them this way puts that energy back into them on some level. Thus, it becomes more possible for them to get back on the journey they intended to have when they came here. Now let's look at some of the many ways our viewpoints are influenced as we progress through our lives.

Science behind Beliefs: The Scientific and Biological Aspect of Beliefs

As children grow up they build the frameworks that define them. Things are viewed from this frame of reference, especially in the formative years, and this molds their view as they grow. As they look at things with this perspective, they continue to create that life; it just builds upon itself, usually outside the awareness that it's strictly their viewpoint that causes their life to be the way it is. This tends to continue until they experience something that impacts them enough to change.

These beliefs are formed. Dr. Bruce Lipton discovered that there is a biologic function that causes further reinforcing of these beliefs. In other words, formulating a belief is followed by a biological/cellular response that helps put these into place within your body on a cellular level. When things happen as you "predict" or "expect," this further reinforces your view of reality and thought structures become more enforced. Dr. Lipton, a Ph.D. in developmental cell biology, found some astounding things in his research that show how this occurs.

In a filmed interview called *Eye of the Hurricane*,[3] Dr. Lipton notes that a cell membrane is basically a liquid crystal semiconductor with gates and channels. Very simply defined, a gate is a circuit with two or more inputs and one output. These allow a signal to pass (or not) when certain criteria are met. A channel is a path or wire along which a signal may be sent. This is also the definition of a computer chip.

The implications of this are tremendous because he realized that a cell and a computer chip were functionally and molecularly the same. He compares the nucleus and genes of the cell to a hard drive with programs in it. The cell membrane is like a keyboard, and the environment is the typist. When the cell goes from one environment to another inputs are given to the cell receptors, which elicit programs from the genes. He concluded that we are a dynamic aspect of the environment and that each human has unique set of keys, like a pin code that distinguishes each of us. The receptors of these pin codes are on the cell surface. Therefore something from outside the physical body is determining the identity of the individual. This means that if something *outside* the cell is determining the identity of the individual, the individual is spirit or consciousness, existing whether or not the physical body exists. We as consciousness exist outside our minds and physicality.

We as spirits decide things. In other words, we as *consciousness* or *spirit* are an influencer of what gets manifested as an identity via the programs of our cells. We are part of the environmental influence on a body. But, as spirits and consciousness, we are also influenced as we interact with factors in our environment. Dr. Lipton further states in the interview

> It started before we were born. A child learns how it fits into the world. It's downloaded. Ideas and data are downloaded into the subconscious mind, especially of a young child, even while still in the womb. This part of the mind is just like a tape recorder: there is no one there monitoring it, or reviewing the content. Commands, pronouncements and ideas are taken literally as vibrational interpretation. The subconscious mind just runs and is a million times more powerful than the conscious mind.[4]

The subconscious mind does not have any concept of time; it is always in the now. He also said, "The life you live is a printout of your subconscious beliefs."[5] With that in mind, listen to what you are saying and thinking throughout the day.

If you combine this influence with the radio waves, news, advertising, microwaves, and the many other factors, it's easy to imagine what a tremendous number of things steer us on a daily basis. Most of this we don't even think about. You can see what sorts of data are being sent to your cells, all of which are living, sentient beings, part of the community of the body. When it is negative, be cognizant of this and change it to a positive thought. Don't continually recite negative chatter. This just reinforces it and its manifestations. Begin to bring it under control. This is tremendously significant, life-changing data that Dr. Lipton cites.

When we look at things they are affected at the quantum level by our energy being focused on them. We are affected by how we look at ourselves. Dr. Lipton's research suggests that cells, operating like computer chips, perceive instructions given to them from the outside, as in thoughts, and they respond with appropriate actions. This shows that what we think is literally interpreted by our cells, and they respond in kind. The entire body renews itself over the period of several years in terms of new cells it creates. Some parts of the body replace themselves on a cellular basis much more often. So, changing our thought habits to more positive will bring about many positive changes on a cellular level over a relatively short time. Our cells can literally have a new perspective reflective of our new thought patterns. Thus, *it is* important how we think. Working on our thought habits and structures over time will bring about change in conditions in our physical state, and these in turn create further changes.

We have discussed beliefs and belief systems, but here are some additional elements to consider regarding our thoughts and the energy contained in them. *This is why it works!* Not only do our cells respond to our thoughts, but there has been much work done in the field of quantum physics showing that the energy of observation changes the outcome of events on subatomic particles. When we look at particles in a quantum world, they seem to change from being a particle to being a wave. The act of observing something changes how it behaves. Numerous experiments have been done with this to demonstrate that it happens. Quantum physics shows they can be either.

In *Matrix Energetics* Richard Bartlett describes a relatively well-known experiment that took place in the late 1800s. This experiment, conducted by British physicist Thomas Young, showed how electrons act differently under different circumstances. He set up an electron beam the width of a single electron and fired it at a wall with two slits in it and photographic plate on the other side. When only one slit was uncovered, the electrons went through and impacted the photographic plate on the other side in a distribution pattern that suggested it was behaving as a particle.

When two slits were open, it went through and the pattern showed that it interfered with itself, thus behaving as a wave. Additionally, when it was *observed*, the distribution pattern on the plates suggested a particle was making the image. However, when no one was observing, the pattern suggested it was a wave.

> But when no one was looking or measuring it produced patterns that were wave-like. So, the inescapable conclusion was that when looking from the level of the electron or photon, the act of observing the electron's path caused it to behave differently than it did when no one was watching it. For this reason the physical character of light was said to be observer dependent.[6]

Gregg Braden references a similar experiment in *The Divine Matrix*.

> Scientists have found that when an electron passes through the barrier with only one opening available it behaves just the way we'd expect it to: It begins and ends its journey as a particle... In contrast, when two slits are used, the same electron does something that sounds impossible. Although it definitely begins its journey as a particle, a mysterious event happens along the way: The electron passes through both slits at the same time as only a wave of energy can do, forming the kind of pattern on the target as only an energy wave can make.[7]

There is another interpretation of this called the Copenhagen Interpretation. Physicists Niels Bohr and Werner Heisenberg, trying to make sense of this in 1927, theorized that the universe exists in a series of overlapping possibilities. These all exist at the same time with no precise location or state of being until something happens to lock one of the possibilities into place. That something is an observation, an awareness focused.[8]

The point of all this is that the energy of awareness can change things. Many possible outcomes exist for situations and individual thought structures. Every aspect of our lives consists of patterns, from our physical bodies to our circumstances at work. There are patterns of thought, patterns at our work, habits, and so forth. It is all light, information, and energy. They all come from our observation and decisions about what they are and what they mean, including our expectations of outcomes and how things will continue. Much of this can come about without paying much attention. All of these things ultimately originate from our thoughts.

When we have a consideration or belief about something, it acts as a basis for further expansion onto these ideas. We tend to view everything around that subject through the eyes of that belief or piece of data we hold to be true. This has a certain vibration or frequency. The experiments with Masaru Emoto and his work with water bear this out.

What We Can Learn from Water

A Japanese researcher named Masaru Emoto has done extensive research with frozen water crystals and the influence of numerous factors on how they appear under a microscope. His books are fascinating, and the outcomes of his experiments totally align with the data presented above. He shows pictures of how verbal expressions, different chemicals, processes such as microwave heating, and reverse osmosis visibly affect the structure of water crystals as they are frozen. Thoughts are vibrations as are different substances. If observation can influence outcomes—as has been shown to be the case—then these experiments further validate this.

The photographs of frozen water crystals shown in his books are very interesting. In *The True Power of Water* (Atria, 2003), he shows numerous water crystals from tap water; water that has been blessed; water that has been given different messages, such as "love and gratitude," "you fool," and "no good"; and water crystals before and after prayers.[9] It is quite amazing.

In these experiments a written message was taped on a bottle of water for a period of time and then frozen. The intent and vibrations of the messages were picked up by the water and the frozen crystals formed in quite different ways as a result of the input they received. The differences are quite remarkable.

The water crystals frozen after receiving messages of

prayer, of love and gratitude, or "you are beautiful" resulted in symmetrical and beautiful crystals. The water that received negative, malicious, or malevolent messages, such as "you fool," "you're stupid," or "I hate you," froze into malformed crystals, being non-symmetrical and deformed.[10]

This is quite important because Emoto notes that our bodies are 70 percent water and a baby's body, when born, is about 80 percent water. Think about the impact of different vibrations present in the water contained within our bodies! In *The True Power of Water* Emoto cites different examples of water being used to treat certain conditions and the outcomes were quite interesting. His experiments, along with the data we know from Dr. Lipton, unquestionably show the value of positive thoughts, words, and vibrations on our thought structures. Being around negative thoughts or giving them to ourselves consistently will have an effect on our cells and our lives over the long term. I highly recommend Emoto's books; they are very enlightening.

Good versus Bad Vibrations

Thoughts are vibrations; they resonate within us. Holding in negative energy, receiving it, or being around it can create a resonance and impressions that have a negative effect on us. It can create a tendency for us to observe things in a way that negatively affect outcomes. Much of our environment contains these factors; often we become rather numb to them and basically shut them out. But these vibrations still arrive in our space. It is valuable if we can be aware enough of them to offset them with more positive thoughts and love. Learn to be aware of energy of the space you are in. Make a point to see how it feels. This ability can be developed just by paying attention.

Since the body is a biological computer and has electrical and vibrational responses to inputs it receives, microwaves and other EMFs can interfere with, influence, and change perception. Chemical substances in food or drinks, as well as prescription and over-the-counter drugs can also significantly interfere with perception and with the body's functioning.

For example, Aspartame (NutraSweet) has a very long list of negative side effects. When this interference happens, ideas can occur to us that might not otherwise. This is how we can be inadvertently steered into feeling a certain way, then set up a thought structure about why we feel that way. These energies can and do trap us more in the body.

There are times when I have wondered what was wrong with me. If you start asking yourself those questions, you'll soon get a list of answers that can cause you to create more similar thoughts. Then you may proceed down that path. Don't go there! It's thought that determines your life. Look at positive things—things you've done right—and look at love. Turn your thoughts around, and don't spend time dwelling on negativity. Thoughts and words program the body computer! Pay attention to how you feel. If you feel bad, you are probably not creating or maintaining beneficial thought structures.

CHAPTER 8
ENERGY AND COMMUNICATION

The Ether

There is another phenomenon that bears discussing: communication and energy flows seemingly through the air without the use of conventional electronics (such as broadcast signals). It has to do with us. We touched on this subject in chapter one in the section called "Connections."

There is an energy field that has been called many things through the ages. It has been studied, described, and talked about for hundreds or even thousands of years by Max Planck, Galileo, Einstein, Sir Isaac Newton and many others. Native Americans and other indigenous peoples have known about this since their beginnings. It connects all things.

It's been called the ether, the matrix, the force, and the field. It is the energy field that surrounds us and is part of us; we are part of it. It is what connects everything in the universe. It is a vast subject and still contains many mysteries. There have been numerous experiments to show that this connection exists and that the matrix is real. There will undoubtedly be many more.

I want to relate one particular experiment that is very indicative of this phenomenon. It begins to show us what effect our thought structures have, not just on ourselves, but the world around us as well. It shows this connection.

This particular experiment was done with DNA to determine if emotions created a response in DNA and, if so, how distance affects the response. It was designed and conducted by the Army with the study results published in 1993.[1] A volunteer subject provided DNA from a saliva sample. The DNA sample was taken into another room and the subject was shown images designed to create genuine emotional responses. Different emotional responses were created with a wide range of images from funny to erotic to wartime images. In each case there was an electrical response from the DNA at the same time the subject experienced the emotion.

The DNA sample was then separated by a distance of *hundreds* of feet, yet its electrical response was instantaneous and coincided exactly to when the subject had the emotional response when the images were shown again. In fact, the scientist that designed this experiment for the Army continued it; he found the results were the same when the DNA sample and the subject were separated by hundreds of miles! The responses were instantaneous; no travel time was required. This implies a connection that has no relation to distance that facilitates the receipt of this information immediately.[2]

This explains so many things, such as how we may suddenly get a perception of something with or without knowingness of what has taken place. We have the capability to literally perceive a "disturbance in the force." In fact, this is exactly what took place on September 11, 2001, and other major events, such as the assassination of JFK. These events can create temporary fluctuations in the earth's electromagnetic fields for brief moments in a magnitude that can be and have been measured. In fact, the Institute of HeartMath[3] has been researching this and similar data since its founding in 1991. The data they have available on their website is very interesting. If all things are connected, which can be easily argued, it has implications on how we are affected by our feelings. It also shows how the feelings or vibrations of others and events in the world affect us and vice-versa. It opens the door to how we can change our world for the better by changing ourselves.

More Messages through the Ether

The following is a description of what is called the "Hundredth Monkey Effect"[4] There is a lot of commentary on this subject, and many have said this whole story is untrue; I bring it up here to simply show how the ether would work. Points made about the results vary from the method of data transfer via the ether, or that when a certain number of monkeys learn something, this changes the balance of what the other ones know. Whether it is true or not, I bring it up here to suggest the possibility of this.

According to author Lawrence Blair's story, there were monkeys living on an island. They were given sweet potatoes to eat. One female monkey washed her potato in the salt water to get the sand off. She showed her mother, who also began doing this. Soon, a significant number of monkeys on the island were doing this except for some older ones. Shortly after this, the same behavior was observed on other islands. The point is, somehow, they picked up this behavior independent of direct communication or contact; there was no way for them to get off the island or for other monkeys to get on. There was no way for these phenomena to have occurred except for the idea that they moved through consciousness via existence of the ether. Communication was sent and received in the form of data through the ether or through intuition and these other monkeys picked it up. That is a natural evolutionary progression. You can do your own research on it, but I thought it was a good example of how ideas and thoughts manage to make their way from one place to another without the benefit of conventional technology enabling it. Have you ever had an idea for a product or service, not done anything with it, and before long you see it somewhere or find out someone else has been talking about it? We can pick up ideas and thoughts this way.

There are a couple of contentions concerning this. One is that information itself can be transmitted through the ether, and the other is that a certain ratio of higher frequency or higher vibrational beings will affect the overall vibration of a much larger number of lower vibrational beings. Both these contentions are related and demonstrate the principle of the ether being a possible medium of transmission for thoughts and information.

Similar claims have been made about humans, that it takes only a small number of highly enlightened beings to offset effects of ignorance and violence generated by a much larger number of people. Dr. David Hawkins discusses this in *Power vs.*

Force. He gives a numerical value of vibrations to different levels of consciousness. Dr. Hawkins gives fairly exact ratios based on his research; this data is presented in a table showing how individuals calibrating at various numeric levels of vibration offset a much larger number of individuals calibrating much lower.[5]

In yet another example of this idea, Gregg Braden gives an example of a group doing an organized meditation that had a demonstrable effect on the surrounding environment.[6] The ratio he mentions is the square root of 1 percent of the population of an area is all that is needed to affect the field of the area. For example, in a city of 250,000, 1 percent is 2,500 people. The square root of 2,500 is 50. This relatively small number of people could create a beneficial effect on the entire population.

The point is we are all connected. Things get communicated non-verbally via consciousness to a higher degree than we may be aware of. We broadcast vibrations and are capable of perceiving and receiving them as well. I share an example in chapter eleven of an energy shift I clearly saw happen in a store I went into. Within moments the energy had totally changed. We can also receive vibrations without realizing it. Working on sharpening our perceptions is a worthwhile effort.

There are other experiments that show an alteration of a substance can occur by the action of viewing it, by the act of perception. As we discussed earlier when covering Dr. Lipton's work, cells themselves sense incoming energy in the form of thought and respond accordingly. The cell receptors act as gates for the incoming data. If you look at this using a computer analogy, the data come in via the keyboard and mouse, and the software program and operating system do whatever they are supposed to do depending on the computer code. So, when we input certain things by having thoughts, the cells respond in the way we are telling them by the vibration from our thoughts. This is why positive thoughts and affirmations work to improve our lives.

Knowing these things will keep you aware of the vibrational company you keep with yourself and with other factors in the environment. Being aware of these points will help you recognize something that comes in from outside that is not you. Keep neutralizing any negative with positive energy until positive is the norm. This universe is alive; it is composed of energy and built upon vibrations. Everything has a vibration. Cells are living, have a level of consciousness, and are adapting all the time. This is a feature of our expanding universe. Life adapts and finds a way to move on, both on a cellular and spiritual level.

Here is a good example of life adapting. A person named Alex had just ended a long relationship. The person he was with all those years was on a different wavelength and, though they got along well, they were not on their desired paths. Their life together had been beneficial for both of them for a long time but had run its course. What brought them together had passed and, even though there was still tremendous love remaining, there was much missing that they both wanted. Each of them had different goals and wanted different things. Rather than continue the stress of living under these conditions, they mutually decided to go their separate ways. Alex was physically drained and tired. He had been steadily losing energy due to the relationship. He began having sessions with energy healers to restore his strength. During this time he was exercising outside every day and riding his bike. He looked forward to this time daily and, for some reason, was eating a lot of salmon.

Months later, during an energy healing session, the practitioner asked what had been going on with his heart. He looked puzzled and said "Nothing that I know of." The practitioner replied that what was showing up was that he had been undoing heart disease and his heart had gotten much stronger and was doing fine.

Now, the interesting thing is that Alex never particularly liked salmon. It was something he would eat if there was nothing else available but it was not something he would ever choose otherwise. For some reason, it just started sounding and tasting good to him, and he began eating it nearly every day. It is high in omega-3 oils and is excellent for the heart. His body just began craving it, knowing it was needed.

This is an example of what we and the body will do when there is something we need. It is cellular wisdom. If we are getting an idea over and over again, it's probably something we need to pay attention to. There is a message we need to listen to.

CHAPTER 9
ENERGY FLOWS:
GETTING RID OF NEGATIVE ENERGY

Relieving Stress

I mentioned earlier the effect of stress on the body and some experiences I had demonstrating that. It is important to get rid of stress so it is not creating problems physically and spiritually. Many times we experience the sensation of stress in the third chakra, known as the solar plexus area, located just below the rib cage. This is one of the energy centers of the body. Anxiety is frequently felt around this area.

There are ways of flowing energy and stress out of the body. Of course, physical exercise is one of the best ways to direct stress out of the body, but there are a couple of other ways. Visualize connecting a hose or a wire to your body in the solar plexus or, as I have done, at an area of pain. Direct the stressful energy to flow out of your body via the tube or wire into the ground, or connect it to a pipe or pole that is grounded. Picture the negative energy flowing from your body into the ground, or just picture it running out of your body onto the ground and away from you.

I have gotten so I can feel when negative energy is present in me or I am just in the line of fire of it. When I feel this I direct it into the ground via a visualized wire or hose. In past instances I have felt negative energy arrive in my direction, and I immediately created a picture of it being captured or deflected and redirected into the Earth. I used the image of a satellite dish-type structure catching the energy and flowing it through a cable into the ground. By doing this I was relieved of this energy, instead of letting it arrive, becoming introverted, and then wondering what was wrong with me. This can be repeated if needed.

Energy can be flowed in, out, or held in the body. If it is held in, it can accumulate in various locations in the body.

Here is something that happened to me involving suppressed emotion and the resulting held-in energy. I had just made a big change in my life. I was writing a journal of all the things I was going through; I was doing this so I could see my progress and how my viewpoint was changing. I was doing lots of exercise and a significant amount of energy work and emotional realignment. I was trying things I had not tried before because I wanted to move into new and different life. This experience took place in my apartment.

One evening I felt a rapid onset of a tremendous pain in my solar plexus area. The pain was intense, and I was more or less incapacitated. I didn't know what was happening. I was just about to go the emergency room, but I couldn't move enough to get up and drive. If you know me, it would have to be pretty bad to even consider going to a conventional hospital without getting some other treatments or opinions from an alternative practitioner first. At the time this happened, I was with a friend who is an energy medicine practitioner. She took a look and determined that there was a tremendous amount of accumulated pain held in place for many years that was finally being released. We worked on this massive amount of emotional energy and guided it out. After that I felt fine; no pain and no further manifestations of this kind have occurred since.

I had been riding my bike, working out, and changing my diet. I had done a complete makeover of my life and was focusing on new routines. I was looking at things in a different way, and not holding energy and emotions in anymore. I was allowing myself to feel, where before I was holding everything in without realizing it. This is a particular problem for men in our culture because we are taught not to show much emotion, grief, or disappointment and "be strong."

This energy was an accumulation of negative energy over many years: the death of two parents, a divorce, my kids moving away and not seeing them for months or even a year at a time. I had been holding on to all this and it was coming out. The practitioner that was with me could see a large black ball of energy, and we went to work and moved it out. This illustrates how the body often has things go on with it that are outside the symptom-categorizing realm of conventional Western medicine. I was in the mode of healing after this lifestyle change and letting things out, having learned about this and getting on a different schedule and diet. It was pretty amazing.

There are countless examples of this kind of thing and how it works. The body is an amazing organism; it has innate knowing and abilities and does adapt to things. It is important to pay attention to it and not to worry and think about bad things. Just know that it will take care of itself if it is able to. Most certainly this *does not* eliminate the need or value of conventional medical care. But I have known many people who go to the doctor for every little thing. This could be because of how they direct their attention throughout each day. This can result in many negative physical side effects manifesting as a result. It has been beneficial for me to learn about nutrition and focus on keeping myself healthy as priority.

SECTION 4:

NEW DESTINATIONS: WHERE WOULD YOU LIKE TO GO?

CHAPTER 10
REACHING PAST THE SCIENTIFIC

Intangible Truths

Science is concerned with what is tangible. While there are many tangible things about this universe, there are many intangibles that are completely possible to experience. These things may be part of other universes or dimensions that are intersecting with our universe. They are merely overlapping or interacting with this physical universe but are primarily non-physical or vibrating in another world. There are many things our physical sciences can't explain or measure. Thus, there are many phenomena and occurrences out of the realm of being provable with physical evidence, since they themselves are not of the physical dimension and cannot provide such evidence.

There are frequencies of both light and sound we cannot perceive with our five senses, but reaching outside these senses could open up more areas of perception. As spirits we have additional perceptions. Refusing to acknowledge their existence limits our perception by putting a thought structure there to shut it off. Love isn't particularly scientific or measurable and neither is intuition, but are they any less real? All of these things influence our thought structures and what we consider valid and "real." The behavior manifestation can be seen physically but, as powerful as love is, it is a non-physical force.

Emoto showed that the water he tested responds to vibration like everything else. It is energy and vibration itself. Negative will produce negative. The efforts to discredit his claims are merely ego-based attempts to be right or to diminish his findings. And it probably does prove Dr. Wayne Dyer's contention that "When you change the way you look at things, the things you look at change."[1] I saw Dr. Dyer say this in a presentation he was giving on a public television show. He had heard it long ago and did not remember who had originally said this. It is profound and it is true in my experience.

We can view this many different ways, but the fact is different viewpoints and vibrations produce different results. This is why different coaches get different results with the same players. Someone who doesn't believe or is skeptical will change the outcome of an observation, especially if their motivation is to disprove or invalidate. Some people get well from supposedly terminal illnesses. Unexplained medical miracles happen all the time. Why? How can they happen? Science or medicine has no explanation, but there must be one if a condition was terminal, or obvious one day and gone shortly thereafter. Something big shifted somewhere!

It is okay to not be able to explain everything! Look for

new explanations instead of trying to make an old one fit. Using meteor showers, electrical storms, swamp gas, and other data to explain extraterrestrials come to mind. Having to acknowledge the existence of extraterrestrials would introduce a whole new set of things to consider, so it is usually dismissed by many scientists. But looking in a new direction is much more expansive and ultimately more productive though less safe than maintaining the status quo.

While there is validity in testing and seeing that things work as represented, there are other areas where this practice will only obscure actual discovery because of disbelief or the act of altering the outcome due to the observations themselves. This is an example of a belief that is a certain way and the new data that arrives being interpreted through the eyes of the person holding the belief. If I have a belief about something, I will tend to find things that support that belief. This is an extremely unproductive practice, unless you are trying to create new beliefs, and the thing you find supports the new belief. This is important to know because we tend to do this unconsciously. Thus, we can expect conflicts in these areas when this is occurring if it conflicts with the truth. It can be difficult to be objective in these cases, but really there is no reason not to be at least objective with ourselves within our own minds. No one need know.

Being Wrong

There is an ego factor operating in our society that has to do with being wrong. No one likes to be wrong. Being wrong undermines our perception of ourselves, and society plays on this a great deal to influence behavior. If you are proven wrong, you often will never be permitted to forget it. This is especially true in the public arena (or in relationships)! But this is an ego function of our perceiving ourselves as a particular identity, and with it having certain expectations. This is something that prevents perception and it really prevents our growth.

If you were out on a golf course practicing by yourself and working on a type of shot, you would expect to make mistakes. They help your body to make the adjustments needed to increase your performance. If you were working with a coach, he or she could use each shot to provide comments and instructive points to help you get closer to the mark. But this is what you would expect. At work or in social situations we frequently feel inclined to defend our positions on issues. We may do this because not having a good defense means we could be wrong. That is equated with failure or stupidity instead of learning. It is okay to be wrong about beliefs if by doing so you are getting closer to the target. Everything is learning on this journey.

Making a Shift

Begin to read things outside your realm of typical thoughts that you have curiosity about. This will get you to look at things in a different way and get your viewpoint expanded to think more "outside the box." That is an overused expression, and we have discussed how we create a box or circle with our usual ideas. It is nothing more than habits of belief and behavior. By expanding our ideas of what is possible, our imagination and creativity is expanded, and we can be more engaged in seeking knowledge. Do some research on crop circles or other phenomena. Stretch your viewpoint! Do exercises or activities that will expand your idea of possibilities. Doing this on a regular basis makes the "box" bigger. Thinking outside it will include things from a wider range of possibilities. You will find things to explore that will lead you closer to your path, or point the way to your next horizon.

There are things going on that are so outside what is normally accepted that no one would believe them. This is how many things are able to continue with little or no scrutiny from the public. There is also the public relations tool of making someone appear "out on the fringe." This is a favorite of the media and politicians, and helps discredit people who are shining a light on subjects the government or some other entity doesn't want to talk about. This is a way to undermine their credibility and get us to cease looking at the seemingly obvious. Why listen to someone "on the fringe"? Make the truth too bizarre and it will be abandoned by most people.

This is done all the time and is simply a technique to get people to not listen to a particular person or group of persons anymore. I have known this technique to be employed, and it is quite effective unless you really pay attention to the ideas the "fringe" person is putting forth and examine them yourself. In other cases, simply making a person in the public eye look stupid or incompetent is all that is needed to get them to be removed from the eyes of the public as credible source of information. As I mentioned earlier nearly all conventional radio and TV stations and print media are controlled by a handful of large media corporations, so controlling a message is pretty easy these days.

I personally know of an individual that this was done to. At one time he was very much in the public spotlight. He is very intelligent and articulate, but had the liability of not being for sale. He was not on the same page as the elitists, those seeking global governance. His reputation was ruined and no one will ever take him seriously again, though he is totally different from his public persona. Ideas too far from the mainstream are rejected by the majority of people, but they have bought into constantly repeated sound bites. So, don't be in the majority. Look and decide for yourself.

Louis Pasteur, Sir Isaac Newton, Magellan, and many other visionaries of their time were all subject to ridicule and harassment, only to be seen as totally correct and brilliant by subsequent generations. Sometimes, these people paid with their lives for being brilliant. The cutting edge is the first to meet opposition that attempts to dull it. You don't have to accept that. Expand your ideas of what is possible. Follow your own path. You may not know where it will take you, but this is part of the mystery. You may spend many years going from activity to activity before finding the ideal circumstance that utilizes all the experiences you have gained. Your changing interest is not a problem in the long run, though you may be told by many that it is.

There is a tendency to look at another person's path as similar to your own, or as something to be compared with your own for the purpose of keeping score. Much in our society is focused on this. We can be big on keeping score. This can lead to evaluation of ourselves through comparison with others and seeing how different we are, deciding that we are better than, or not as good as, others. I have known very "successful" people in terms of creating wealth who were total personal wrecks in the area of relationships or some other area.

There are many parts of a life and everyone has an area of brilliance, something they can do at a very high level that will give them great happiness. It is unfortunate that in our current world, we often do not acknowledge what is really valuable because it does not create a lot of money or prestige. We are a left-brained society, having focused on the head rather than the heart. We are focused on getting people to produce goods and services they can sell by thinking, not feeling. This is the corporate push in the schools to get people who can think, not necessarily feel. There is nothing wrong with thinking, but the left brain is not particularly good at creating; it is best at memorizing, organizing, evaluating, and controlling. It has a *very* small capacity and processing power compared to the right brain.

Creativity has contributed to developing the most innovative and valuable technologies known to man. Our society has been too heavily focused on logic and less focused on imagination and creativity but both are needed. A society's level of morale is determined by feelings. That is spiritual. Look at very old buildings as an example. Watching the Tour de France cycling race, you can see castles, churches, and other buildings built centuries ago. We don't see anything like that now. We are in the mindset (particularly in the United States) of "it takes too much time; get it done as fast and as economically as possible" or "That other stuff looks nice but who has the time? Time is money. " Look at the universe; there is nothing but time! Look at the Grand Canyon. How long do you think that took?

Spending time out in nature slows us down and puts perspective back into our lives. We live in such a fast-paced world; our thought processes are being altered to become shorter and faster. This does not help us in the long run. If something takes too long, we may abandon it.

We can be so programmed to be unconsciously in the mode of conforming that we just fall back into it when presented with circumstances where that's needed or desirable for the time being. It's just better if we are aware that we're doing this, that we're falling back into something familiar, and don't just fall back into it as a habitual thought structure. So many people are comfortable in a narrow range of personal experiences and practices. Getting outside of those mindsets is essential to enhancing our expansion. Sometimes it's not comfortable for a while.

I have been part of this mindset, too, and it was not helping me. After a while my focus got so closed in that my perception of things outside my computer screen or my immediate world was unperceivable. Not good... Sometimes it takes a catastrophic experience to pull you out of this. This can be just a wake-up call to get back to some things that are important.

CHAPTER 11
CREATING NEW HABITS OF THOUGHT:
HOW TO EVOLVE

Here is a Native American parable that I think is profound. It goes like this:

> The Creator gathers all the animals and says, "I want to hide something from humans until they are ready for it: the realization that they create their own reality."
>
> "Give it to me; I'll fly it to the moon," says the eagle.
>
> "No, one day soon they will go there and find it."
>
> "How about the bottom of the ocean?" asks the salmon. "No, they will find it there, too."
>
> "I will bury it in the Great Plains," said the buffalo. "No, they will soon dig and find it there."

"Put it inside them," says the wise grandmother mole. "Done," says the Creator. "It is the last place they will look."[1]

From here, we are going to look at ways to transition to new habits that will help us redirect our lives in the way we want to go. Look forward; don't look back. Every moment is new; every day is a new creation with new possibilities. We are creating it moment by moment. Change your mind, reach out, and experience. Wind down the old stuff. Spend an increasing amount of time doing something for the new you. Spend time being the new you, visualizing the new you. Every time you do this, you begin creating the new world: our world and your world. You are in a constant evolution; just realize it. Remember to be in the moment. The more you're in the moment, the more you're creating the new you. Things will occur to you. Your frameworks of thought structure will shift. The idea that people don't change is totally wrong. They only seem not to change, but they are changing all the time. I have spent many days and often years in recreating myself into the same thing over and over, but there was still change occurring. Then something would come along that was not a habit and things would shift. Then a new model could be created.

Living in Our Hearts, Not in Our Heads

This world needs more love and respect. How can we bring this about and constantly keep the vibrational level higher around us? It is up to us to find a way; developing this ability will help improve conditions around us. Remember that we are all connected. The vibrations we put out are received by other people and put into the general environment out some distance away from our physical bodies. I have found a way that has been effective for me, and you can find one that works for you. I work on feeling love and appreciation.

Think of a time when you experienced a strong feeling of love, affinity, or appreciation for someone, or it could be for a space you were in when you felt love and a peaceful feeling. Memorize that feeling. That vibration is beneficial for you to be able to bring into your space whenever you can. You can also learn to look at others with that feeling.

For me, I think of the love of my children, especially when they were young. I can feel that love and have learned to project that onto others. When looking at other people, I imagine them as a child, innocent and seeking to experience the world—trying new things, learning to walk, riding a bike. I have some favorite pictures of my kids; they are great, memorable times that I look at. When I do, I can feel love for them and the general feeling of love. That is a feeling, a vibration that is very high. Learning to produce and project that feeling at will is an excellent way to continually raise your emotional level to that of appreciation and love. Your viewpoint of everything improves when your predominant emotion is that of appreciation or love. You can look at people you don't know and appreciate them and feel some degree of love for them also, knowing they are on their own path. They are souls like you and have their own issues and life circumstances they need to deal with. Looking at people like this tremendously raises the vibrational level out to a broad area and can even change *their* outlook for a period of time. It helps them (and you).

I feel we must be able to look at people this way for us to make real headway as humans evolving into higher states of consciousness. It is difficult at times but, with practice, it gets easier. You can build it into a thought structure. It all has to do with your viewpoint. Being able to love and be at peace with yourself makes this easier to do with others. They will respond to this in dealing with you in nearly every case because they perceive this on a spiritual level that cuts through the social layer.

Have you ever been attracted to a total stranger, or felt instant affinity for someone you saw or met just because of a look or how you perceived them to be? (I am not speaking of sexual attraction, though that could be included.) Some people you can look at or say "hi" to and it just seems like they would be a good person to be around or maybe spend some time with—that they would be trustworthy, for example. That's what is taking place. In these cases, a person might look at you with some affinity or appreciation and you perceive it on a level outside the five senses. You might think or say, "There was just something about that person" or "I think I know that person." (You probably do know this person from another time.) It is perception. Most likely it is a transmission of how they feel about themselves and others. Small children and animals instinctively perceive this because they don't have all the social barriers in place yet.

You Are the Key

When you can't trust what you see or are taught it becomes difficult to trust anything. But having an open heart, open eyes, knowing yourself and your senses, is the best way to proceed.

Try it. Try trusting yourself. Sometimes you may have to work on this some first. You *are* worth the effort, believe me. There are plenty of things you have done right no matter what you might think of yourself.

You need to learn when you can take your own advice. That takes realizing you *do* know. But you need to know when you're moving in the right direction. Can you trust the perceptions that are coming through? I grew up with datum after datum piled on top that skewed my viewpoint of what was possible. My outlook was often inclined to be skeptical or slightly negative. It was altered to perceive any glass as cracked or half empty. So, when I used to look at any opportunity, my first thoughts were usually, "What can go wrong?" or "How can it fail?" "What are the dangers (from aviation training)?" "Why won't it work?" "How are their numbers wrong?" "What are they lying about?"

I had an expectation things were not as they seemed. (I could have started a skeptic's website!) This is what we have learned due to dealing with a massive and pervasive lack of integrity on the part of people we were supposed to be able to trust. This was a thought structure I needed to identify and overcome without being naïve.

It is important to be aware also that there are still untruths (and rats) out there. They just don't have to be a big or consequential part of your world. I was attracting what I was expecting, based on what I had observed.

I look at a lot of information being presented and find flaws that are often due to the providers obscuring the truth to make it look better. This gets back to integrity and how a lack of it within ourselves undermines our own perception and faith in our fellow man. If we have poor integrity with ourselves, we may look at others as if they are as untrustworthy as we are. It helps strengthen and build out the idea structure that is in place. So we need to be able to create and attract viewpoints and people with integrity. When we do that the rest of the world begins to change. Lack of integrity would be met with scorn more so than now. Now it is more or less expected at worst, or overlooked at best, in many of our previously trusted professions. It is so common; it has been tolerated as a consequence of the way things have come to be in our current society. We tend to gravitate toward people who have the same viewpoints, and these reinforce each other and resonate together.

Being able to trust is important. When you can't trust yourself you have nothing. You can destroy trust in yourself by not being true to yourself, and by not having basic integrity in yourself. Lying to yourself is one of the fastest ways to do this. Try to justify something to yourself that *you know* not to be true. Repeating the story over and over will not make it true and you will know it. But it is important to recognize this.

It is okay to be truthful to yourself. No one need know the lie you told yourself, the underlying reason you did something or took some action. For example, if the real reason you did something was not really to help someone, but to make them think better of you, then seeing and acknowledging this is being truthful to yourself. If you still helped them, great, and if they thought better of you, that's all right, too. But be honest with yourself and your integrity and perception of integrity will rise as well. Standards will improve in your environment, and you will not attract those with a lack of integrity. You'll feel them a mile away. This will bring about a change in our environment.

I have thought about this when it comes to looking at my own honesty. It has helped me sort many things out. Standards will improve in your environment if self-honesty increases, and when you look at things, the change *in you* will create other changes. If more people start doing this, our world will shift in a more positive way. In fact, it is already happening.

Even people who are not generally respectful of others will respect some people more than others. There's a sense outside the five main senses that causes them to do this. (There are many more than five senses by the way, including sense of time, perception of the sun's position, and more). This has to do with self-perception and how that person looks at others. People can feel who they should and should not be honest with. There is a perception that causes them to do this.

When kids are young they are more creative and imaginative, and we may lose patience with them after a while. A common viewpoint is that while they are young, it is okay for them to spend a lot of time engaged in their minds and imagination. Yet, as the years go by, we have less patience with this and expect them to conform with our left-brained orientation. This is not helping us as a society. Albert Einstein framed this brilliantly when he said, "The rational mind is the faithful servant and the intuitive mind is the sacred gift. We have created a society that honors the servant and has forgotten the gift."

I have had a great deal of difficulty trying to solve things using a strictly left-brained approach. For example, flying is mostly a left-brained activity, though the *love* of flying is mostly a right-brained activity. I got into flying for the love of it.

The rules, regulations, and obsessions with procedure—to the point of continuously focusing on the potential dangers—

spoiled much of the pure joy of it for me. Of course, there is a great need for standard procedure and standard actions in most things, especially aviation. This is to be expected and is fine. But in general to obsess on disaster chronically focuses attention on it. I just think most things would be better if we believed more in imagination, and if it were accepted and we weren't so mired in practicality. This limits us and makes the current physical universe more rigid because we grant it more importance. The fabric of this universe is set up to be much more accommodating than we think. (Those left brainers may argue heavily with this)!

Be good to yourself, and be good to others. If we all did that, we would be in a different place. Truth and integrity are the best ways to improve this world. I know this works; energy changes where this is used. If you look at things differently, people in your environment will respond or different people will wind up in being in your environment. Everything responds to love, even machines and other things we don't believe are alive. Even those things are composed of light energy and information at their quantum level. There has to be structure and order, but this can be accomplished without so much destruction of each other and our dreams. Live and let live. There will always be some who will want to destroy and attack, but they don't have to be part of your world. Let them be attracted to people who expect and want to experience that. There are plenty of those people around.

Here is something I experienced one time where the visible vibration changed as a result of me feeling very exhilarated. I had just finished a long meditative session and was feeling incredible. I had a feeling of love for everyone. I was totally exhilarated, happy, and felt totally expanded. I was outside of my body. I was aware of a large sphere of space around me. I was with a friend and we went into a convenience store for something. We were laughing and talking. There were only a few people in the store: the clerk and several others. None of them were smiling or talking. Within minutes, the whole space had changed. The clerk was laughing, and joking with a customer that was checking out. The other customers were smiling also, looking at us having such a good time.

Our vibration had changed the vibration in the store within a couple of minutes. It's just a feeling of happiness and exhilaration. We have all seen a baby laughing and seen the effect it has on the people around him or her. A baby is very recently arrived from the non-physical plane and carries much of that fresh, beautiful energy with it. This energy and its vibrations influence the surrounding space in a pronounced way. We all can do this when in a state of true happiness, exhilaration, and appreciation. We do influence our surroundings as they influence us. Knowing this makes it more apparent why it is important for us to be in a high vibrational state of appreciation. We can learn to control our own vibration/emotions most all of the time.

How does this affect the way you deal with your everyday work? I sometimes get stuck on something and then try to use logic to fix it. But I have a habit where I just list down what is wanted, then imagine ways to do it but oftentimes there's no follow-through after that. I just put those notes in a file and, boy, do I have a lot of those! There have been times I would just go off and meditate on it or go for a hike in the mountains or a quiet space, and see if something else pops into view. That has seemed to work for me. I put in the request, and then I let the right brain work on it. I may come up with some ridiculous things first, but usually something useful results. As Abraham says, problems are on a different vibrational level than their solutions.

I realize how many conflicts and misdirected thoughts I have had, and trying to discover solutions often leads into a circle. You can do it. You have infinite ability. You just need to realize that ability is there. Tap into it. Step outside yourself and, even if you do this a little at a time, that is a gain. I often feel I am somewhere else, and then snap back to this location. When I get back, it seems like everything has shifted somewhat and the perspective is different. There is so much going on that I can't inspect it all. I need to just let it flow. Every ninety minutes or so, we go into a state where the right brain tries to get more engaged and let recent thoughts consolidate and use what information has just been absorbed. This occurs sometimes as a sleepy feeling. When that happens, get into that zone for a short while and see what results. You will be more productive. (Especially if you don't overpower this state with coffee!)

Self-Development: A Meandering Path

I want to tell everybody that they are appreciated and valuable. Each person has something to give; each person is on a personal path that will serve them somehow. (I know for some people that is difficult to believe!) Some people move faster than others and progress on their path in great leaps and then do nothing for a while. Great leaps happen when some event or realization takes place, so putting yourself into a place where this can be brought about will be beneficial. It's also beneficial when there's nothing going on so you can have time to reflect and review your life progress. I think of my journaling and how valuable it has been in helping me organize my thoughts: I see how fast I am evolving and how it is going. It is amazing to me sometimes when I look back and see it. I began journaling when I was separating from a marriage and making a transition in my life. I had decided to simplify my life. I gave away most of my possessions just to be able to start anew. I was operating with the idea of getting a career going where there would be lots of income potential and a way to help people and build a business.

I had decided to build upon my finance background and decided to become a financial planner. However, after getting involved and seeing the actual nature of the work, I realized it was not what I wanted to do. For me, the way to find out about something is to just do it for a while and see how it goes. I don't think there's better way of finding out about something than just doing it for a while to experience it, though that's not always possible.

After getting through some of the classes, I got a good picture what I would be doing. I paid some visits to a few financial planners and realized that the stability and professionalism is what I admired. They always knew what they would be doing the next day, and that has an element of security about it. It can make one feel safe. They make good money if they have enough clients, but it takes a lot of clients to get to that point. It also takes time to get them. This is fine; I was comfortable with working hard and always have been. The thing is, after getting all those clients, they can never go anywhere for very long, or do anything else. They are completely tied to their clients, and many financial planners have so many it may be difficult to serve them very well. (They do take good care of the big ones.)

I considered this characteristic and then recalled the time I spent skiing; I could not continue on the financial planning path. I am too restless a spirit to get welded to an office or location. I've always needed to be active and outside doing things. Being completely tied to an office and location seemed like a trap to me. But the features of having consistent work and stability had appeal. All this was for me was being able to have something I could be proud of, the appearance of it, that is. This originated from a thought framework I had. I was raised with the viewpoint that this was important and the key element to our identity.

Studying something can help you determine if there's any interest in the first place. But, even then, the occupation is likely to be quite a bit different than you thought once you actually begin doing it. But, each time you find something you do not want to do, you will know. At the very least you will gain experience from doing it and nothing will be wasted. Yet many times, parents, friends, or associates may imply you have failed or you can't find your niche. This is simply not true. Many times it takes numerous experiences to determine what you really want to do. It has for me. All this is part of your path. It is important you see it this way and not the way others may view it. I steered myself into many "careers" after having adopted the expectations of others. I felt I had to live up to certain expectations of my family and peers. I took this on, correctly or not, and created thought structures as a result that I've had to discover and undo. It is a process and part of the journey.

This is so different from when I dropped out of college to ski. All I wanted to do was ski. As I mentioned earlier I went on a ski vacation over Christmas break and did not return to college. This began a great adventure, and I was perfectly happy to just ski all the time because it was what I wanted to do. There was perfect focus, nothing else in mind.

After some years, though, the thrill of it subsided and the reality of earning a living loomed overhead. I was doing fine working construction in the summers and waiting tables or bartending during ski season, but I was growing tired of doing that. I quickly realized that I needed to do something else if I were ever going to acquire enough money to avoid living week to week. But this sudden need to do something else also coincided with a spiritual shift within me. I was questioning where I was going in life and what it meant. This was in the 1970s. Often when there is a career or relationship shift or other significant life event, there is a catalyst for questioning and self-examination. I felt a renewed need for a spiritual quest. A coworker was pursuing his own spiritual search, and we would talk extensively about ideas and questions along those lines. I wound up getting involved in a series of spiritual studies again to find out more about what my current life was all about and my role here. I had nearly always had a belief that I was a spirit and that I had been here before. Finding out more about this possibility had much greater appeal than the religion classes I had attended in college. It was a search for information about the nature of life and us as spirits.

All these classes and retreats cost money, and I could see there would be a continuing demand as time went on. It is probably normal to wonder how things would have been different had I pursued a different course. But I believe things happen for a reason, and we direct ourselves into those areas where there is something we need to experience. What would have happened had I continued to work in the ski business that I loved? I might have wound up working for one of the ski corporations in some department. I had been a ski instructor and, though I enjoyed teaching, I was so focused on my own progress I did not really want to work at instructing. I may have continued using "recreational substances," though, and things might not have worked out so well. It is hard to know where that path would have led. It is difficult to look back and know where a path would have led. We can speculate but it's mostly an unknown.

But I got into this course of study and decided I needed another career that would be fun, one that could eventually produce a greater amount of income: being an airline pilot. I thought this would be a good career, be fun, and eventually provide a decent living. What happened was that many airlines had gone out of business at that time and there were plenty of highly qualified and experienced jet pilots needing jobs. I was competing with them.

Where does going for money instead of following your dream lead? It seems that many things can become confused, and it may be easy to abandon your dream, put it off, or dismiss it as just that: not valid, not properly aligned with your concept of "responsibility." After all, we live in a world where we need to make money to survive. As Jack Welch, the former CEO of General Electric, said, "You need to eat while you dream." This is true, but it is too easy to abandon dreams amid the demands of our society's thirst for "practicality." The best thing to do is figure out some way to keep a hand in the dream while planning how you could shift into the dream and what it would take.

At that time my dream had shifted into attaining higher awareness and spiritual knowledge. I was seeking enlightenment and had become intensely interested in who I was as a spirit, what my abilities were, and what I was doing. Looking back, I had many gains and good experiences, as well as many bad ones, but I believe my spirit chose that path in order to get away from using recreational substances and alcohol that were widely prevalent in the ski scene.

This spiritual study and training created a whole new set of thought frameworks that were useful at the time but only within the framework of that group. I did not see this until later. Many problems derived from these thought structures surfaced over the next few years and continued for quite a while. As a result of these beliefs, I spent years discovering how many misperceptions I had created and how much I had missed by holding onto these ideas. There were positive things, including an expanded awareness and perception of life outside this physical dimension and the body, as well as greater ability to look at what was possible. I had moved "out of the box" on much of my thinking, and this has helped with the further spiritual study I have done in the years since. I had also stopped using "recreational substances." It also indirectly got me into the financial area because by then I saw what was happening in the aviation business and that it would be a long time before I would realistically make enough money to live well. At the time I had a family and bills to pay.

I was attracted to the financial markets because of the

opportunity it provided, but also the fact that it is a constantly moving game. Though I did not view it as such at the time, I also felt a need to do something that would be well thought of by my peers, an ego-based thought structure still intact from my upbringing. This need to be well thought of was simply my not being aware of my spiritual identity. There's nothing wrong with being well thought of, but having a *need* for that can be a liability and can cloud your decisions. These are patterns and values not based on a long-term spiritual perspective. I had forgotten this and been steered into accepting importances that were not essential for my spiritual growth. This is something I see clearly now. There were "good reasons" at the time for doing all those things but, ultimately, much of my true purpose was lost, buried, or at least misdirected for a time.

When re-finding a purpose, or becoming aware that you have strayed, your purity of choice will be affected by the thought frameworks you have accepted and put into place. It is important to see this and know it when it reveals itself. You might not find the exact thing that expresses your current purpose right away. There may be other things you wind up doing first, but nothing is wasted: it is still experience. It will most likely turn out that having that experience serves you well in any new directions in which you find yourself going.

Getting involved in the market and trading was good for me for a long time. It was very enjoyable overall, but there was a factor that had to do with my expectations, what I believed would happen. What I wanted and what I actually *believed* would happen were often different, and this needed to change. I continually needed to create the new story and begin to believe it. This is thought structure orientation. There was the belief I would be successful, but often there were temporary conflicts between desire and expectations. These interfere with clear choices and directions. It is always a work in progress. It is developing a skill of creating new thought structures and seeing when old ones are a hindrance. I am always "renovating" from a thought structure point of view. This has been the biggest area to shift in my thought process, noticing the difference between what I *wanted* and what I *expected* would happen. I would think, "I really want this, but probably…" And then I would fill in the blank with a lowered expectation.

Being aware of these conflicts, and just how pervasive they are, has helped me to see how slow I was going. I put things off. There were conflicting worries that just slowed progress into something new. Things I read, or would hear about that were basically unknowable, caused hesitation within me and contributed to indecisiveness in moving forward. These ideas also ignore the concept of creating our own reality and the idea that there are many possible outcomes from any one scenario and that we are instrumental in creating them. In short, I worried too much about things out of my control. I also wanted to make the best possible decision in everything. This is also unknowable to a large degree because the quality of decision is arbitrary in many cases, and it depends on other outcomes that occur later.

So I needed to stop worrying about things and start creating. Second guessing yourself is rarely productive. What would have happened is usually unknowable. I believe dwelling on these is a waste of time and negative creating. These types of questions create procrastination and make it easy to retreat back into doing what is familiar and comfortable on a daily basis. By creating a new story, I am painting a picture and putting myself in it. That is what makes sense: creating my own sense of who I am and what I should be doing. Also doing my part to contribute to others' growth where I can—putting out the example of my experiences and what I have learned from them—is important. When I read a book or attend a seminar, it shifts my thinking, and often old thought structures crumble and fall away. Some structures shift and realign. This makes way for new ones just the same way that a fire burning in a forest hillside makes way for new growth. It is all the evolving of the universe and of us.

I look around and realize there is no scarcity of stories to tell, and there are no reasons not to tell them. In the past I constantly evaluated myself and how I was doing. This is the problem with our society and the thought and value structures we have in place. Without paying attention, we can inadvertently become subject to these evaluations. They do not serve us or our society. We are on our own paths. We often get pushed into having very short time horizons and comparing ourselves to others. This does not help us.

CHAPTER 12
REMOVE THE BRAKES,
REMOVE THE BOUNDARIES

Viewpoint Shifters: Some Concepts to Entertain

What if we all were to have the viewpoint that we were timeless beings, and we were either coming back to this world or a similar one the next time we returned to physical form? What if we were able to look at each other as fellow travelers in the universe and that we were all connected? We are all part of the entirety, the plant and animal kingdoms, those who we disagree with—even our enemies—as well as those we love. There are things about ourselves we might have trouble with, hate, or disagree with. What if we were to have the view that when we see or hear something or someone we dislike, it's a mirror of something in ourselves and those things we dislike about ourselves? Is that actually what's happening? See if you can find something like that in yourself. You probably will. It is okay if you do. No one else needs to know but you! Be honest with yourself, despite what your ego suggests.

It is true that without everyone having this viewpoint there may be "our enemies" who would take advantage of us with our guard down and destroy us. But, if we create our world individually, over time it will be such so that those individuals won't show up in our world because we no longer resonate on that wavelength. This is why people eventually drift apart, their vibrations and resonance shifts enough so mutual interests and attractions change. How often have we thought or heard, "he's changed" or "she's changed." It is probably not personal, but rather due to people being on their own paths. Sometimes people are aligned for a period of time, but eventually they find another direction. It is normal; don't take it personally! Maybe it provides a catalyst for you to examine your own path.

What if you could take the time to learn something or do something with no regard to how long it took, how it would be accepted, or whether you had time to pull it off before some other thing had to happen? How would that be, to just do something for the purpose of mastering it and not worrying about the aspect of time or acceptance?

This is how animals operate. They just live their lives according to what their instincts are. They don't worry about if they will be on time or accepted or do the right thing. They just are. It is beautiful, and you have to admire and love them for that. They have much to teach us in this regard. We could do much better if we operated with a much closer connection to nature but, with our world the way it is, this doesn't work for the most part. There is always some deadline, some obstacle to be met. Our society is just very disconnected from this viewpoint, and we need to reconnect.

Not long ago I asked for divine guidance in figuring something out. Shortly after that during a meditation I clearly received the following communication. I think it applies to many situations, which is why I have included it here. Though this communication was via thought, I receive similar guidance when journaling.

What matters is that it's effective and created by you so you can see it, agree with it, and follow it. Where you go off the rails is when you try to follow someone else's system, you have disagreements with it, and don't then really follow it. This was something created by someone else, and they have a different thought framework and a different view. Take in that data, but make it your own; use what you can see works and makes sense, and disregard the rest, or at least remodel it so you can use it with no conflicts. You'll have belief and positive expectations that way. This is what creates worlds. Follow your own intuition; it is all you need and will serve you well if you allow it to do so.

This advice has been profoundly useful.

An example of what used to happen with me is that I would get some information or read in a book and wind up agreeing with part of what was said but not the rest. Then I wouldn't figure out how this could work for me, or what parts of it could work for me. I was adding to conflicts I already had in place because I didn't recognize existing thought structures that conflicted with the new information. Now I usually do see it and can feel those earlier ideas crumbling away and my "database" realigning. Sometimes I will actually see the time and place I received the information that has just been rendered invalid.

I recently recognized a conflict I had held for a long time regarding money. I grew up with the idea it was not particularly desirable because "people with money were not the nicest people" and that "money wasn't everything." In this case, it was the opinion of my mother, and it was just another thing "wrong" with my dad. They were divorced when I was young.

These viewpoints that she had in place were a result of her experience. I did not feel one way or another about money when I was a young child, but I have seen this had an effect on my consideration of it later in life. That feeling about money in general conflicted with my perception that the constant need for it was a threat to my freedom and what I wanted to do. So the ideal thing would be to find something that is enjoyable that will bring in money as a result of doing that activity. And, in fact, that is the ideal. Doing what you want to do is the way to happiness while on your journey. My mother said, "We don't have those choices" (when, in fact, we do).

However, I adopted her belief as my own at that time without questioning it. This caused a conflict within me, and at the same time served as a justification for not making enough money. That was probably the exact same way she was using it. Take all things in proper context. It is no crime to be well paid for what you do in line with the value. It is a natural thing and part of the exchange ebb and flow of the energy of money. It keeps things balanced. What I have found is that there are incredibly nice people with money, just as there are rats with money. And there are incredibly nice people without money, and rats without money. Money by itself does not determine whether someone is a rat or not. The determining factors are values, integrity, and character—or lack thereof.

In their books and CDs, Jerry and Esther Hicks cover this concept extensively via their non-physical friends and advisors called Abraham. I have found their books and CDs to be very helpful and enlightening. They have published many books on the Law of Attraction and the power of deliberate intention. Here is a quote from a CD included with their book *Money and the Law of Attraction*[1] explaining how the story you are telling manifests:

> The more you beat the drum of anything, the more you activate the essence of it in your vibration. The more it is activated in your vibration, then the more the Law of Attraction is matching you up with things like it. And the more the Law of Attraction is matching you up with things like it, the more you observe it. And the more you observe it the more you talk about it. The more you talk about it and observe it, the more you beat the drum of it or offer the vibration of it. The more you offer the vibration of it the more Law of Attraction matches you up with it.[2]

And so on, over and over. It is a cycle. Use it to your advantage. Create a new story, and come to believe it.

Learning to Create Appreciation

For nearly every barrier we face, there are ways to dissolve them. Learning ways to effectively remove these barriers helps us create a continuing story we can believe. Then the whole thing gathers momentum. The only way to do this is to trust in yourself. There is no better viewpoint than your own judgment. While it is true that we all need experts to advise us and we cannot know everything, we can know ourselves and our feelings. Get the information from whatever source you need, then use your heart and judgment to decide. We have been trained to look at data and not feel with our hearts. Believe me, I have had data tell me one thing and my heart tell me another, and I should have gone with my heart's feeling nearly every time. Trust yourself. Learn to love yourself and appreciate yourself and you will be able to appreciate others more fully, too. By appreciation I mean having a sensitive awareness, and recognizing the value (especially the aesthetic value), of something or someone. Doing this will help them and will improve the state of our world, even though it might not be readily apparent at the time.

I can even appreciate people I wouldn't have been able to years ago, even though they are doing things I don't necessarily approve of. They are just doing what they see as best for them and probably don't look at a big enough picture yet. They may have conflicts and integrity problems and my seeing them for the essence they are makes it more likely they will eventually be able to resolve these conflicts. In the meantime, I focus on creating my world one moment at a time.

I am often successful at staying in the moment and creating, but it takes daily practice. I remind myself to do this. It is like eating right. If you gradually eat more and more meals each week that consist of what you should be eating, there will be improvement; it will become the norm. You won't likely be able to do it all at one time and you don't need to. There are thought structures in place, and there are habits that need to be changed and turned into a lifestyle. When you get to that point you will begin to experience a great amount of success because new constructive habits are in place.

Another reminder on changing thought structures and habits: don't beat yourself up if you slip. It takes practice and patience with yourself. Learn to appreciate yourself more. One way I do this is to see myself when I was younger learning things and going through life. I look at myself from the present day back to those days. I see the struggles, the fun, the problems, but mostly I look at how I was trying things, learning about life, and growing up. I look at the experiences I had, things I could be proud of, and events that made me smile. I look at happy things, I see pictures of me taken at various stages of my life, and this helps me appreciate myself more. It is really important to learn to love yourself. Forgive yourself, too. Don't dwell on tough times. It is not necessary or helpful. You can look at them, but just remember it is important to look at what went well and how you have gotten to this point. From here, you can continue to create.

Though it is more beneficial to stay in the moment, there are things to be learned from occasionally looking back in a certain way. You will see where you have been, and you will begin to see where you picked up the thought habits you have along the way. This is a good way to see how they got there and how you acted at the time. I don't do a concentrated backtracking and review anymore. It was not very effective at creating change. I work to improve my mood and appreciation for myself.

Most people can really feel some love and affinity for a child. I can do this by looking back at myself. I have found this technique very helpful in producing the feeling of love and appreciation for myself. This enables me to feel appreciation and love for others I don't even know. There is not enough love being brought out in the world, and this helps. I am not talking about ego-based pride, but rather a feeling of genuine love and appreciation for how *you yourself* have experienced things, made your own way, and weathered adversity; this is *real* appreciation for yourself. It is a very high vibration, and the more time you can spend there the better. Being able to produce this feeling within is immensely valuable. You will be able to appreciate others more. Until you can appreciate and love yourself, your love and appreciation for others will be compromised or nonexistent. All things considered, you are quite awesome! And you have huge potential.

Other ways I bring out this feeling in myself is to look at the pictures of my kids when they were young and experience the love I felt for them during different times of our lives. It is the simple act of remembering things that were fun. It is interesting that earlier in my life I would look at these events with a feeling of slight sadness knowing they were in the past. It was a pattern and came from a viewpoint that things would never be better than that. This was not my viewpoint but was one I had adopted from another prominent person in my life. This was just something I was doing. I was putting that emotion there. It was a habit and a thought structure and, when I realized this, it just disappeared.

A few people I was constantly around while growing up were sad people. These people did not perceive their lives as happy, so they would look at the fun times in the past and be sad they were gone. They tended to look at everything that way, and I just adopted this without really knowing I had done so. When I realized this I started eliminating that way of looking at things. There was no real sadness in those events for the most part. Maybe their sadness came from their current lives, and looking back just reminded them of that. Either way, it was a thought structure for me that I spotted and I decided right then it was entirely unfounded for me to simply look at those past moments with a melancholy reminiscence. After that, I started focusing on the fun things my family and I were planning in the future, or focused on enjoying the moment. Now, when I look back at those times, I do not get the melancholy aspect. Remember that the current moment is the most powerful because it is all there really is. You create your future moment by moment.

Being in the Zone, Getting in the Zone

Have you ever been really in a zone where everything flowed smoothly and you looked at things that might be difficult and, because of the way you felt, they seemed easy? That is because everything depends on your viewpoint. If all is not going well, even the simplest thing seems difficult or aggravating. This also can occur when you are tired. Clarity is a function of perception, of being in the moment and operating from a high vibration. This will enable you to perceive at a much higher level.

When I'm in the zone it is amazing. Traffic lights turn green as I approach them, and everything goes effortlessly. If I am having a difficult time, it is just the opposite, and everything is frustrating or annoying. You have probably experienced both of these states.

When this occurs, I have some key memories to look back on and things begin to smooth out. I can get myself back to feeling good. Get back into the moment. I take the time to improve my outlook. Sometimes it may take a while, depending on what has happened. Create some calibrating thoughts for yourself that you can use to get yourself back into a high and constructive vibration By calibrating thoughts, I mean a "go-to" thought, which is a memory that you can recall easily and that will put you in a better frame of mind by recalling how you felt then. This is a technique I use whenever I need it. If you are having trouble with this, shut off all thoughts for a short period and recalibrate. It is beneficial to learn to do this. And, when you have moments when you feel really good, make a mental note of them; "bookmark" them so you can add to your list of calibrating thoughts.

I remember a time when I was preparing to compete in a skiing event. It was a championship at the end of the season, and I was feeling quite good, in excellent shape, and it was a pristine day. I will never forget this experience as I had such a high degree of clarity. It was a mogul skiing event, and I was practicing a few days before the competition.

At the start of one run I saw the entire course—every turn, all the way to the bottom. I had the whole thing in one view. I had never experienced that before. It was the best run of my life. Too bad it was in practice! But there was no pressure; I was relaxed and enjoying the day. It is moments like these that you should "mark" and remember because they show you what is possible. Use moments like that. Everybody has them, even if they seem few and far between. Work on getting into this feeling more of the time, and do it consistently, so that it becomes a habit and a new way of living. Your viewpoint is everything. It is the creator of your world, and it is available to you at each moment of each day. No matter what is happening, there will be another day (or another life). Enjoy each moment or at least be aware of each moment, and know you are creating your life, right now.

In the 1980s I spoke at seminars about the power of visualizing things we wanted to see happen and of positive thinking. On breaks I would usually have someone come up to me and explain how positive thinking did not work for them. This was their thought structure and they didn't seem to notice it was working perfectly! We are creating what we chronically think of. These people didn't see that they were creating the condition whereby positive thinking did not work for them. They did not expect it to. That was a thought structure they had firmly in place. Maybe it was helping them explain some other problem. Often people cultivate weaknesses or frailties in order to escape something in their own lives, and it is quite possible they aren't really aware they are doing it.

Thought structures can be subtle, but don't discount how many you have. Don't think badly of yourself as you discover them. As you discover them they tend to dismantle themselves. Be happy and realize this is the growth process. Be glad when it occurs. When you become aware of these things, many other things will shift in your mind that you can't necessarily see at the time. Just know the process is working; you are becoming more aware. Continue! You are a sacred being, and you should realize this. You have many abilities that are probably not being used. Trust yourself and love yourself. Work on making this a habit.

There are many techniques to improve your outlook and build better thought structures. Getting in physical shape is good. It helps your overall viewpoint and can help you move toward a goal of losing weight or just being more active. I prefer outside exercise whenever possible; however, depending on where you live, there may be seasonal problems with that. If you can get outside anyway, that is a good way to go. If you live in a city and not much nature is readily available, try to find a park or peaceful place where you can exercise. Gyms are my least favorite because they do not have the most beneficial aspects of nature and fresh air. But using my iPod with good music I can still focus and enjoy it. I have had great workouts in gyms, too.

Exercise activity helps our viewpoint become more constructive. Exercise releases endorphins, which the body naturally produces. Endorphins are hormones that produce a natural high. Exercise also helps the body cleanse itself internally via the lymphatic system. After I have gotten into an exercise routine that I can continue (and enjoy enough to continue), I get excited to go exercise. I go for walks, hikes in the mountains, and bike rides. It gives me time outside to be in nature and observe animals, birds, and the terrain, and it is an excellent stress reliever.

For me, if I don't like the exercise, I have trouble continuing it. In order to make lasting changes, it is important that you adopt habits that you can sustain long enough for them to become effective. It is possible to do something for a short period of time that may be beneficial. If I don't like a particular exercise, I allow other things to get in the way. This pulls me off my routine. If you can find something that will make you happy—creating it as more or less a permanent lifestyle change—you will be likely to continue it and have it be part of your new life. If you are feeling better and creating good lifestyle changes, your thought habits and structures are rearranging into something sustainable. This in turn will increase the momentum for further changes and improvements.

Voracious reading is another thing that I found extremely helpful. Reading new ideas will help you find things in your environment that can be improved and give your mind new frameworks to evaluate. I always have a good list of books I'm working on, and I don't worry if sometimes I spend time reading fiction. This helps, too, because there are things in every part of your day that can help you build on your perspective. I tend to avoid a lot of TV because it is agitating to my state of mind with all the advertisements, and just the content itself usually creates negativity. I noticed how I felt after watching TV: my energy was lower and disrupted, but I wanted to keep watching! It is fairly addictive. I am not perfect, but I have found little changes can be made that reduce stress in the environment—creating one that is more conducive to expanded and constructive thought. Making little changes that stick and become routine are in fact steering you onto a different path. Small changes can turn into big results or give you the momentum to make better changes, so don't discount them.

Reading many different books that address similar subjects or address them in a different way enables us to get a more complete picture and formulate a better understanding of a subject. As we continue to read and explore more data, we are adding to our database. More things will align as they are also combined with our experience. It builds upon itself. As we become more able to perceive, more possibilities occur to us. George Bernard Shaw once said, "Life isn't about finding yourself. Life is about creating yourself." We are creating our lives either knowingly or unknowingly. Remember, life is a journey. We are in a constant state of change, as is the universe, and we are part of it. It is important that we are aware enough to know when we are being truthful to ourselves. There is no substitute for it.

Also, continuous reading and learning keeps our thought structures in a continuous state of evolution by increasing awareness and expanding viewpoints. Becoming aware of more things greatly enhances our ability to find creative solutions to things. Learn to be more aware of how you feel in order to determine how you are doing. Continuous reading and learning is valuable. I read things that I am drawn to because this has frequently been the best way for me to find something I had been looking for or show me a path to it. Sometimes I'll buy a book and not wind up reading it for a while, deciding to read something else first. I find one book leads to another, and they usually work out to be in a good sequence. If nothing is resonating at the time, I read fiction. That will usually get me interested in the next subject. But I have created the habit of reading every day.

Many TV programs and print media outlets play on our fears and keep us in that vibrational level. Living in a state of fear makes us more vulnerable to disease and reduces overall well-being. No doubt you can see how being in a state of fear makes you liable to see things quite differently than you would if you were relaxed and free of stress. I'm not saying to be unrealistic in the perception of our world, but there needs to be a balance. Whatever is happening right now is the result of earlier thoughts. Realize that when we are fearful or worried, those are the signals we are sending to our cells. Those are the lenses we are looking through when we view the world. That won't help us rise above the disruptive potential of events that may be occurring. It is tough sometimes to realize that we need to do certain things to improve our situation if it isn't desirable. But understand that life is an evolution; it continues, and great things can come out of bad or any less-than-ideal circumstances. The very act of changing our viewpoint and starting to consider ourselves lucky can help eventually bring this about. Think of what you are creating from moment to moment; get an idea of this and the potential.

I worked with a guy long ago who had a tattoo on his arm that said "Born to Lose." What a surprise when it turned out to be true! This guy constantly told me story after story of his misfortunes through the years. At the time I was much younger and had not considered the connection between thought structures and outcomes, but his "bad luck" started with his thought structure. *Then* the evidence came that confirmed to him it was true.

I had this backward for a long time; I thought the circumstance was first, *then* we reached a conclusion, but it's the other way around. First is the persistent thought and then the event. First is the thought/vibration, *and then* comes the outcome if the thought pattern/vibration is repeated enough. "I'll believe it when I see it" should be "I'll see it when I believe it." I just wasn't perceptive enough back then to understand this. Although events *can* occur first that may initially get you into this thought process:

Event → thoughts concerning it → conclusion → belief → thought structure → more thoughts like those → more and continuing similar events and this whole thing begins reinforcing itself.

For the most part, the thought comes first in some way, and the rest follows and repeats. Thought is the beginning of creation. Continued thoughts about the same thing result in manifestation.

Trying on a New Reality

Break into new ground and get more involved in finding things out. This expands awareness and helps us move on our path. You will be drawn toward those things that will help you move on this path; many of us are drawn to different things. Don't worry about how long it takes; look at how much time nature takes in her cycles. There's no rush; everything happens in its time. We are inundated with the frenetic pace of our world. This is not helpful in getting us closer to ourselves and becoming more aware. Learn to be still; create some time to yourself often and meditate. Quiet your mind, and then things can come in. Our pace today differs so much from nature. The seasons go by seemingly fast but there is an order to it. Nature's pace has much to do with us, but we often do not listen and go with the flow of life.

Here is an example of a massive shift in life priorities and how they can rearrange us. Sometimes this happens because of a significant or traumatic event (perhaps in our own life) that totally rearranges our reference points on what is important. The movie Castaway,[3] with Tom Hanks, is an example of such a huge change in priorities compressed into a short time. I had seen this movie long ago and recently saw it again. My viewpoint on life had changed a great deal since the previous time I saw it.

In the movie Tom Hanks's character works for Federal Express, and his priorities were in line with that job and its demands. It was all about time, schedules, and deliveries. During one flight, in literally minutes, his world changed radically from being engaged in society and working for a shipping company to being stranded on an island far from anything else. His priorities shifted about as far as they could in a short time, and he had to create something else at the start of each day. He was stranded on the island for a long time. At one point he decided to leave the island, go out to sea, and take his chances there. It is an excellent movie for trying on a massive viewpoint shift, and also for contemplating putting yourself in the hands of the universe.

It gave me perspective, got me to look at what types of things are really life changing, and how I would react in that type of situation. It would have been really difficult. Yet seeing this rearranged some of my thought structures about what is important and things I could change about my life. The idea of love basically got him through this event and led to his recovery. He totally surrendered to the elements. He had a plan; he just did it and it wound up working. Had he not built that raft at the time he did and drifted into the location he did, he would have been in an entirely different situation. So he followed his own guidance about getting off that island. Yes, it was just a movie, but we do have help with our guidance; we are not alone. If we let it in, amazing things can occur. But first we have to let this guidance in.

Follow your own guidance. Your guidance is probably the most perfect thing you have to make decisions with. The way to make it even better, stronger, and more trusted is to eliminate those things that make you second guess yourself, things that interfere with clarity. If you feel happy when considering a direction, it is probably the right thing. Conflicts and beliefs discussed earlier play a big part in this, and the thing that brings these about are our responses to our environment: what we see and the way we see it. This is a key to understanding how you can change your life at any given point. Life is changing all the time: cells are dividing, our bodies are renewing and maintaining themselves, and the stories we are telling ourselves and others are coming into existence. However, even though this is happening constantly, many people don't realize they are constantly changing into the same thing repeatedly by telling the same story and giving themselves the same model repeatedly. One popular saying goes like this: "The more things change, the more things stay the same." I saw myself doing this at different times earlier in my life without realizing it. This is basically the construction of a rut! Use this process of continuous change to move toward the more ideal life you want, not just recreating the same thing over and over.

Learn to be at peace with yourself; don't second guess yourself because you have been right many more times than not. Take a look at times when you second guessed yourself and changed your mind. Or maybe there were times you were talked into changing your mind about something. If you go back and look at these, you'd probably find that you could have trusted yourself to make the right decisions about most big things. I have seen this many times in my own experience.

I did not take my own advice and often this was or became problematic. Had I followed my own consciousness or gut feeling, I would have been much better off. Many times I have also taken the easy path, and this didn't always turn out well. The other path might have been scary or unclear or risky, so I went with what was right there. Sometimes it worked and many times it did not turn out as well as it could have. Sometimes you begin down a path that doesn't end up working as you planned, but there is always something of value you can take away from the experience. Follow your own advice. It is fine to get the feedback of others—particularly if they have expertise in a particular field—but ultimately you need to make the decisions and know they will be right. This is your path; your intuition is your guide and it is appropriate.

The bottom line is you can make changes; they can be very beneficial and can happen quickly, but get the noise out of your way. There is so much noise in our world. It is really beneficial to frequently go to a place that is calm and peaceful. Let your mind become quiet. This will allow more things to drift into your awareness. That is a way to steady improvement, and it is vital that you do this or find this place and make it a regular occurrence. Get exercise, every day if possible—at least something. Listen to your inner guidance. Keep your eye on the big picture, something you want to move toward and keep going. Challenge yourself, love yourself, and build on this constantly. There is no end to unnecessary details, so keep going on what you are working toward and don't get bogged down.

Affirmations: Tell a Story

Here's an example of a guy I know well—we'll call him Ben. At the time we began discussing goals and accomplishments, he told me some things that I was able to sort out with him and improve his effectiveness at achieving what he was working on. He was experiencing a pretty good life, and nothing was really going wrong. But he wanted to be better at what he was doing, so he was spending an increasing amount of time on it. He was not really getting anywhere because he was always second guessing himself. He could see this was because he had been taught that failure or being wrong was unacceptable. He had often been ridiculed for failure in the past, so he just never put himself in a position to fail. He continually played it safe. He never made himself fully available to experience and therefore learn. He decided this viewpoint had to change as it was obstructing his progress. He could see that failures and being wrong are key ingredients to learning. Conventional wisdom tells us that we don't really fail at something until we quit completely. Edison failed to make a light bulb thousands of times before he was finally successful.

Ben realized it would be helpful to create an idea of what he wanted and continually repeat it and visualize it. However, his new story was built from the viewpoint of things that he *did not* want to happen. So his focus was from that orientation and, whenever he was in a position where he felt good, he would hurriedly make some affirmations that would be designed to keep him free from the things he did not want. Everything was done from a defensive stance. This made little sense. It reduced the effectiveness of his affirmations, and it was puzzling to him why they were not working as fast as he wanted them to.

This is because of the conflicting belief (resistance) he had in himself and in the nature of the affirmations.

He would play them over and over and hoped it would sink in to his subconscious. He would listen to them when he was asleep or taking a nap, or even while meditating. They actually had begun to work to some degree. He could see some progress, but now he needed to improve the focus and the purity of his affirmations so they weren't approaching things from the idea that they might not happen. His belief in this was real, but he was tentative. There was more hope involved than *knowing* these affirmations would materialize. So his affirmations were done from a viewpoint of *asserting*, and *hope* instead of belief.

He was still not really making himself available to create his life through his affirmations. Ben would write down these affirmations after doing a meditation when he felt powerful and in a very high vibrational state. His thought was this: since he wasn't always so positive he had better put these things down and hope they would stick during times when he wasn't doing so well. He was hoping or wanting a certain outcome but it was not what he actually believed would happen.

Instead of this approach, we looked at doing things from the viewpoint that they will happen, or that they have *already happened*. They needed to be more focused and put in direct alignment with what he wanted. If they were aligned with his intentions and projecting the idea that they were in fact happening, then they would be fully realized if he would just get out of the way. I told him about my experience with the airplanes, and how when I was there sitting in them, I was focused on the fun of it and seeing it happening, not thinking it wouldn't or worrying about when it would happen.

So he revised his story and his affirmations. He worked out his plan and aligned his energy so that he was feeling in the zone every day for at least a good part of the day. He finished his plan and realigned his strategies toward something he really wanted to do anyway, because he enjoyed working out solutions to his conflicts. After doing this, he could function without his previous conflicts, and he was able to use the new data he discovered. As a result his job performance improved markedly.

He had looked forward to this better performance for a long time. It had come to him in bits and pieces but consistent success had been largely elusive. His dreams are now being realized on a daily basis and he is using all the tools he has to get more and more productive. He is able to pass on what he has learned and is really having more fun all the time. He is helpful to people and proceeding on his own path at an accelerating pace. And the most positive thing is that he is doing what he wants to. His energy is in a positive state of change and he created all this by realizing, evolving, and getting his own resistance out of the way so he could follow his dreams.

The reason I was able to help Ben discover this is that I had done a similar thing myself years ago. I noticed that I was making affirmations from a similar viewpoint. I would repeat things over and over that I wanted to happen with the idea that, if I did it enough, it would overcome the feeling that they probably *wouldn't* happen. I was making affirmations from a state of hope. I would also put in some extra things and repetition for good measure, hoping that would overcome me actually having to be there and believe (because I didn't).

I was willing to believe. I could talk myself into what I wanted by just making sure my story was straight, but I wasn't really convinced. I didn't see how much different this methodology was from the airplane event when I wound up flying those airplanes. There it was just fun, no resistance. I knew I would have to do some work in that direction as well. I don't expect things to simply show up unexpectedly (even though they have many times in the past). I was doing affirmations with the knowledge that my thought structures needed to change. I had not changed them so far, and they seemed to be stubbornly in place. I thought that making and repeating affirmations would overcome the underlying belief while being somewhat doubtful it would happen. I was subtly acknowledging it probably wouldn't work; that thought structure was held in place. It was all based in hope.

This was my experience with affirmations and my thoughts about them. This was an example of conflict between my belief and my desired outcome, and me not seeing they were worded from an expectation that something unwanted could continue. This was not being in the moment and not believing fully that my affirmations would work. I was hoping they would work, but I was "not getting my hopes up."

Trusting that affirmations work is separate from visualizing how you want things to be. Affirmations work. When we are unhappy with the way things are and keep noting this to ourselves and others, those are essentially affirmations. Think about it: if we are constantly going over something and acknowledge that's how it is, then we are doing the basic action of an affirmation, even though it's not something we want. We are repeating something in our mind and/or explaining our situation to others. If things are staying the same in our lives, this unintended affirmation is working! That's the biggest reason things are staying the same.

The guy at the seminar who kept telling me positive thinking did not work for him was continually affirming this. And he was right. The actions I was missing were just to visualize what I wanted and imagine it being there, without deciding or believing anything else about it. It was a pattern. The pattern (thought structure) needed to be changed. Edison kept affirming the existence of the light bulb. He just kept seeing it in the physical world. He believed it would work.

Now I can tell when I'm not certain about my affirmations and I get the conflicts out of the way. Remember the words Abraham mentioned earlier: "The more you see it, the more you talk about it, the more you talk about it, the more Law of Attraction matches you up with it, the more the Law of Attraction matches you up with it, the more you observe it …"[4] It's just a loop that replays. It is a thought structure. Commit to your story, affirmations, and visualizations. Things and circumstances will begin to occur that will bring about the change you desire. Remember our discussion in an earlier chapter about how the universe works when we let it.

This was a tremendous discovery for me. It is also seeing how to be responsible for results and participate in life by making myself vulnerable and willing to be accountable. This means you are really in there playing the game and willing to win, lose, or draw. You are really playing, and that is the key to being able to create change. If you lose when you weren't fully playing, the loss was tolerable. If I won, I would say "great," maybe quit, have the trophy, and be able to say I did it. I can look back at that viewpoint and see how integrity was missing somewhat. I was lying to myself a little. *The act of commitment realigns things!*

This following quote from W. H. Murray, a Scottish Himalayan expedition member, puts this fact into perspective.

> Until one is committed there is hesitancy, the chance to draw back, always ineffectiveness. Concerning all acts of initiative and creation, there is one elementary truth, the ignorance of which kills countless ideas and splendid plans. That the moment one definitely commits oneself, then providence moves too. All sorts of things occur to help one that would have never otherwise have occurred. A whole stream of events issues from the decision raising in one's favor all manner of unforeseen incidents and meetings and material assistance which no man would have dreamt would have come his way.[5]

We must be practical, but there is a limit to its usefulness in the soul since our concept of practicality is based on our current world and perceptions of it. It is a left-brained activity and therefore limited from a growth perspective. Getting too oriented or locked into your everyday world is limiting. Your perception will begin to be dialed back.

There are credible arguments that the world or reality as we see it is an illusion, that it is a hologram being created by us as we go along. I believe this is true, and I have experienced instances where I have seen this. But when I get too focused on organizational matters or day-to-day production, I seem to exclude some perception. I am too busy; I don't perceive subtle things just outside this physical world. When in the mountains or in meditation I do perceive more. I work on extending my perceptual reach outside this physical realm.

Learn to feel more and think less. We have gotten away from feeling with our hearts into thinking with our heads.

In the movie *Enter the Dragon*, martial arts master Bruce Lee admonishes his student and instructs, "Don't think... FEEL."[6] Change your point of perception. Don't automatically invalidate some perception or idea because it's unusual and you don't have an explanation of how it could be real.

Simple Exercises to Try

These are some exercises I have done that have helped expand my viewpoint. As a spirit not restricted by a body you can do these. Don't worry about the specific technique of how to do them; just do them without concern about whether you are doing them correctly. There is no "correct" way. I have purposely omitted any instructions as I want you to just do it how you think you should go about it.

Change your point of perception. Look at your town from up in an airplane. Look at an airplane flying above, and then imagine being in that airplane looking down at where you are. Look at the moon from the Earth. Now, look at the Earth from the moon. Gradually expand your view: imagine looking at Earth from another star. Again, *don't worry about the mechanics of how to do this, just intend to do it and see what happens.* And don't worry about "how you did" with that exercise. Don't judge your performance. You may feel like you have left your body momentarily. Don't worry: you are connected to it, but it is not you. It is just the body you are working with in this lifetime. It will be fine and so will you.

There are abilities you can develop if you just look and don't rule out or negatively critique what you experienced. Break out of the structure of this "reality" that we take for granted. Also, spend time being quiet and just shut off all thoughts. If an angel were to communicate to you, how would you perceive it? Would it be a voice, a concept arriving, or a moment of clear knowing on your part? Would it be a tremendous feeling of love all of a sudden? You might experience all of these at different times, so it could be any of these.

One thing that happens to me regularly while writing in my journal is that the context changes. I will be writing about something that has occurred or that I am wondering about and the writing shifts into an answering mode. It begins to change from the viewpoint of "I" into the viewpoint of "you," such as "you need to try doing this..." or "you need to put your attention on ..." When it changes to "you" it is worded like guidance, just like the example I gave earlier as a divine guidance that came to me in a meditation. It is as if some guide is sending me thoughts and they are received through my writing. I looked back through my journals and "you" just appears in paragraphs here and there after I am writing (and wondering) about something. It changes into a form of guided answer in these instances. I was very amazed when I noticed this. I had not noticed this until after attending a workshop on angels and spiritual guides. It is very consistent, and the guidance is always valuable and pertinent. This is one of the many ways we can be communicated to by angels. Answers to our questions come when we ask and then watch or listen for it. It may also come in the form of a repeating thought.

Dr. Doreen Virtue has written many books about angels. In one of her articles she brings us this message from Angels.

> We aren't that difficult to hear if you will listen for Angel messages with an open heart. Most of the time we are closer to you than you can imagine. A whisper, a thought, is the only signal we need from you to get

a conversation started. We have enormous respect for what you're going through here on planet Earth at this time. We never seek to interfere with your lives, only to bring you blessings of insights and new ways of looking at yourselves.[7]

The answers I have received while writing in my journal seem to validate this.

Here is another exercise to try. Sit quietly and get the feeling of totally being able to trust. Look at the practice of apprenticing or mentoring. What if you could work with someone who would honestly teach you and make sure you knew everything you needed to know about the thing you were studying? There are no time constraints, no agendas, no untruths, no holding back of information, and no misleading. How beneficial would that be? What would that feel like? Memorize that feeling. With perfect integrity this would be the way it would be done. People would be more trustworthy and competent. The world would be a better place. It would be incredible, and there would be great results. In some cases this does happen, but in other cases it does not. Integrity can't be legislated into existence. Neither can trust or respect.

There are other realms we can contact or be part of, and not seeing them does not mean that they are not there. One such course that can get you started on expanding your perception and abilities is called "Mindscape." More information on this can be obtained via the website: www.bodytalksystem.com/learn/mindscape/. Doing a Matrix Energetics seminar can also help create new perceptions. If these seem interesting to you when you research them, you might consider participating. I am sure there are other seminars that are beneficial also. I have done many different seminars, and there is something to be gained from all of them. If one seems to attract your interest, then there is most likely something you will gain from attending.

Journaling

Personal journaling is a valuable activity for me because I can see how things evolve from day to day. It allows me to see the growth and the change, similar to how pictures or time away from a growing child allows you to see the change in them. I recommend this highly. Being around a child every day makes it difficult to see the magnitude of changes in them because they occur while you are there. If you only see them occasionally, the changes seem more pronounced. The same thing occurs with us. Since we are always with ourselves, we might not see the changes that are occurring. This was certainly true with me.

After ending a relationship, I began journaling and noted the attitudes and thoughts I was often immersed in. As I began doing things on my own and discovering new things, my habitual attitudes and thoughts began changing and I could see this in my journal entries. Now when I look back at those journals, the amount of change over a relatively short period of time is huge. I would not have noticed this without journaling. I could see the progression of thoughts and how my thought structures were changing. Journaling also accelerated this process by making it clearly visible. It was a way for me to step out of the day's events and note my thoughts. I could see that the main orientation of my thoughts was changing. In addition, I have received considerable guidance in the form mentioned above that has been very helpful.

We can recreate ourselves over and over in the same mindsets, and this is one reason they appear not to change much (And, in fact, they are not changing much). The cells in the entire body are replaced quite often depending on the part of the body. The point is our bodies are constantly renewing themselves. Those cells are receiving input from us as consciousness. If we focus on noticing what is different as we begin expanding our horizons, we will see revision and realignment of thought structures taking place. We can make physical and spiritual transformations. It can be a real adventure, and we will most likely be allowing ourselves to gradually return to a path more closely aligned to the one we came here with.

Here is an example of how feelings can set up thought structures and how they can evolve combined with energy. This is something that would become visible through journaling. You can more easily recognize patterns as they were developing or as you were getting rid of them, by writing them down as you become aware of them.

Being Aware of Energy

One house I lived in had a set of marks in the inner spine of a folding closet door. Whenever my boys would visit, I marked their heights on the door in pencil along with the date and name. I did this for years and it was always a point of love I could look at. I did not see them often; they were with their mother out of town, and she was not able or willing to have them spend too much time with me. So I cherished this time. It was an emotional event for me when I finally sold the house. So much living goes on in a house over the years. That energy you can take with you, and it can be either beneficial or harmful. In my case here, it was sadness at having to leave this behind.

It is important to expel negative energy, but remember the positive if it enhances your viewpoint and how you feel. I memorize how I feel during good times then I can recall it. It is an emotional state or vibration. These are the types of things that can add to thought structures in a beneficial way or destructive way in the case of negative energy. Ideas or comments you think then come to believe like, "It was in that house that I really lost my sense of direction," or "it was in that house where I picked up this: _____" (fill in the blank) get repeated. They can easily become a belief. Other points then begin aligning around it, confirming that this is indeed the case. This is how thought structures are unwittingly built, as we have discussed.

Energies can also remain in a building and be perceptible. They can be the energies we put in or they could be left over from earlier occupants. This explains how sometimes being in a certain place has a "good feel" to it. It could be a house, restaurant, or any other building. There is energy there to some degree, and it usually is perceived on some level by all of us.

Dwelling on misfortune is wasted time; it holds you in a field of negative energy that will attract more of the same. It is one thing to note mistakes and see they were mistakes, but to go back and relive them over and over strengthens negative thought structures. Remember Abraham… "The more you observe it, the more you talk about it, the more you talk about it…" Having "field-tested" this principle myself A LOT,

I can attest to its truth! Practice moving yourself out of those types of thoughts. When they come up, work on being in the moment; put your attention on all that is happening right now. While sitting in a chair, feel all the parts of your body that you are aware of at the same time. There is so much going on each moment, but we often are lost in our thoughts.

Thoughts or observations we make in a particular situation may cause us to reach a conclusion or decision about something that then becomes part of our thought architecture. We begin to see everything with that qualification. It can be very subtle, but then other similar thoughts get added onto it. We can begin to operate using this data as it has become a conclusion and a belief. The number of ideas we have like this is astounding, and they accumulate and influence our paths. Remember the story I was told when I was in school about not being good at math. I believed that one for years, and it altered what I believed I would be able to do or not do in my life.

Conclusion

In conclusion I want to emphasize the key points in this book. Be honest with yourself. You are on a path and are part of the fabric of the universe. The universe is expanding all the time, and it has a memory that we are a part of. It is important to realize this when you are driving to work, at home, or any other of the many things you are involved in here on Earth. Have a broad view of yourself in the context of the universe. You have tremendous value, even if you have not realized or acknowledged it yet. If you have acknowledged this, please never forget it. You are adding to the experience of the universe.

We are spiritual beings animating a physical body. We can get caught up in this to the point we forget who we are and what we have in the way of abilities. Comparing ourselves to others and judging ourselves is easy to do, but it is not helpful. There are many ways to expand. Don't hold negative energy, and don't get caught up in building on ideas you have taken on that are not serving you well. You really don't have any areas of incompetence, except for those you have decided on or quit working on. Maybe you have good reasons (and that's okay), but know that with some work, you could pretty much do anything you wanted to. You have no limits.

Become aware of the ideas you hold, especially those that imply a lack of ability. See how you might have contributed to their construction. Be aware of the continuing process of building such thought structures and reducing your abilities. Know you are creating your life at each and every moment; try to be aware of each moment. Work on spending time in the moment. When your mood changes or something happens that causes you to move off your path, be aware of it and remind yourself of who you are.

It is my hope that you learn to expand your abilities and wind up on your path. I hope that you really enjoy the ride of this physical experience because it can be fantastic. We are constantly growing and meant to grow; that is what the universe is doing, and we are part of it. Spend time being outside, preferably in a natural setting, and walk, ride a bike, or do something that helps you to focus on nature. Nature is tremendously healing and beneficial. Learn new things that are outside your area of normal pursuit if you have interest there, and let it lead you to other things that will be beneficial. Find places where there is profound quiet (except for maybe the wind), and spend time there allowing your mind to relax and your intuition to flow.

Treat yourself with respect; you are an infinite being, regardless of how it might seem on any given day. Realize your path is an evolving thing and it is meant for you to grow.

Everything that happens is an experience you can learn from. Having this viewpoint will help you make the most of it. There are a vast number of loving, helpful, and well-meaning people on this planet. People do not always agree but, for the most, part they mean well; after all, they are trying to create their worlds, too. Often they may conflict with yours, but most everything can be worked out. Governments, organizations, or individuals may have an agenda but, if you are focused on your own path and are in a high vibrational state, misfortune will pass you by. You just won't be home when it calls. Why do some people survive the worst disasters when others around them are destroyed? There is much about the energy of this universe we do not understand. The possibilities are endless. Stretch your mind!

I wish the very best for you and hope you have a great ride!

ENDNOTES

Chapter 1

1 http://en.wikipedia.org/wiki/Akashic_records#cite_note-0.

2 http://www.crystalinks.com/akashicrecords.html.

3 Braden, Gregg. *The Divine Matrix: Bridging Time, Space, Miracles, and Belief.* . Carlsbad, Calif.: Hay House Inc., 2008. Page 16.

4 *The Sixth Sense*, Written and directed by M. Night Shyamalan, Perf. Haley Joel Osment, Bruce Willis, Olivia Williams, Toni Collette. Walt Disney Studios Distribution, 1999.

5 *Dragonfly*, Directed by Tom Shadyac. Perf. Kevin Costner,Susanna Thompson, Joe Morton. Universal Pictures, 2002.

Chapter 2

1 http://www.quotecollection.com/quote/losers-visualize-the-penalties-of-failure.

2 *Orbs, The Veil is Lifting*.   Produced by Hope Mead & Randy Mead. Beyond Words Publishing Inc & Merkabah Productions Copyright 2007.

3 http://www.goodreads.com/quotes/show/987.   Albert Einstein quote.

4 *Star Wars, The Empire Strikes Back*, Directed by Irvin Kershner. Perf. Mark Hamill, Harrison Ford,Carrie Fisher, Billy Dee Williams, Anthony Daniels. Twentieth Century Fox, 1980.

5 *Ibid*.

Chapter 4

1 http://thinkexist.com/quotation/the_thing_always_happens_ that_you_really_believe/155539.html. Frank Lloyd Wright quotes.

2 Icke, David. *The David Icke Guide to the Global Conspiracy (and how to end it)*. Isle of Wight, UK: David Icke Books Ltd., 2007. Page 512.

3 Hicks, Jerry and Esther, *Ask and It Is Given: Learning to Manifest Your Desires*. Carlsbad, Calif.: Hay House Inc., 2004. Page 309.

4 Bidinger, Sandy, http://www.practical-personal-development-advice.com/whatisenergy.html.

5 Bartlett, Richard quote, during a Matrix Energetics workshop, 3/12/11 Phoenix, Arizona.

6 *Ibid.*

Chapter 5

1 Hicks, Jerry and Esther, (The Teachings of Abraham). *Money and the Law of Attraction: Learning to Attract Wealth, Health, and Happiness*. Carlsbad, Calif.: Hay House Inc., 2008. Page 205. This part of the book was a transcript of a Law of Attraction workshop held in Boston, Massachusetts, on Saturday September 29, 2007.

Chapter 6

1 Hicks, Jerry and Esther, (The Teachings of Abraham). *Money and the Law of Attraction: Learning to Attract Wealth, Health, and Happiness.* Carlsbad, Calif.: Hay House Inc., 2008. Page 205. This part of the book was a transcript of a Law of Attraction workshop held in Boston, Massachusetts on Saturday September 29, 2007.

Chapter 7

1 Bartlett, Richard. *Matrix Energetics: The Science and Art of Transformation.* New York: Atria Books, 2007, p. 18.

2 *Ibid.*

3 *Eye of the Hurricane, .* Producer/Director, Elizabeth Richter, A Video Interview with Bruce Lipton Ph.D. DVD, 2007.

4 *Ibid.*

5 *Ibid.*

6 Bartlett, Richard. *Matrix Energetics: The Science and Art of Transformation* . New York: Atria Books, 2007, p. 65.

7 Braden, Gregg. *The Divine Matrix: Bridging Time, Space, Miracles, and Belief.* . Carlsbad, Calif.: Hay House Inc., 2007, p. 72.

8 *Ibid.*, p. 74.

9 Emoto, Masaru. *The True Power of Water: Healing and Discovering Ourselves.* New York, Atria Books, 2003, pp. 51–82.

10 *Ibid.*

Chapter 8

1 Motz, Julie, "Everyone is an Energy Healer: The Treat V Conference," Santa Fe, NM. *Advances: The Journal of Mind-body Health* Vol 9, (1993).

2 Thompson, Jeffrey D, D.C., B.F.A., online article, "The Secret Life of Your Cells," Center for Neuroacoustic Research (2000) . This article refers to the work of Thompson's colleague Dr. Cleve Backster and a book about Backster's research of the same title. Website: www.neuroacoustic.org/articles/articlecells.htm

3 http://www.heartmath.org/research/research-home/global-coherence.html

4 Blair, Lawrence (1975). *Rhythms of Vision: The Changing Patterns of Belief*. London: Croom Helm Ltd.

5 Hawkins, David R. *Power vs. Force: The Hidden Determinants of Human Behavior*., Carlsbad, California: Hay House Inc., 2002, p. 282.

 6 Gregg Braden. Lecture on youTube http://www.youtube.com/watch?v=HvdfFW-yYGE&feature=endscreen&NR=1, "Ancient Understanding of The Heart Field."

Chapter 10

1 Dr. Wayne Dyer, youtube.com Apr 19, 2008.

Chapter 11

1 Icke, David. *The David Icke Guide to the Global Conspiracy (and how to end it)*. Isle of Wight, UK: David Icke Books Ltd., 2007.

Chapter 12

1 Hicks, Jerry and Esther, (The Teachings of Abraham). *Money and the Law of Attraction: Learning to Attract Wealth, Health, and Happiness*. Carlsbad, Calif.: Hay House Inc., 2008.

2 *Ibid.*

3 *Castaway*, Directed by Robert Zemeckis, Perf. Tom Hanks, Helen Hunt, Paul Sanchez. Twentieth Century Fox Distribution, 2000.

4 Hicks, Jerry and Esther, (The Teachings of Abraham). *Money and the Law of Attraction: Learning to Attract Wealth, Health, and Happiness*. Carlsbad, Calif.: Hay House Inc., 2008.

5 Murray, William Hutchison. *The Scottish Himalayan Expedition*. J. M. Dent & Company First Edition (1951).

6 *Enter the Dragon*, Directed by Robert Clouse. Perf. Bruce Lee, John Saxon, Jim Kelly. Warner Bros, 1973.

7 Virtue, Doreen, http://www.angeltherapy.com/article13.php.

BIBLIOGRAPHY

Bartlett, Richard. *Matrix Energetics: The Science and Art of Transformation.* New York: Atria Books, 2007.

Braden, Gregg. *The Divine Matrix: Bridging Time, Space, Miracles, and Belief.* Carlsbad, Calif.: Hay House Inc., 2007.

Dyer, Wayne. *The Power of Intention: Learning to Co-create Your World Your Way.* Carlsbad, Calif.: Hay House Inc., 2004.

Emoto, Masaru. *The True Power of Water: Healing and Discovering Ourselves.* New York, Atria Books, 2003.

Richter, Elizabeth. *Eye of the Hurricane.* Producer/Director, A Video Interview with Bruce Lipton Ph.D. DVD, 2007.

Hawkins, David R. *Power vs. Force: The Hidden Determinants of Human Behavior.*, Carlsbad, California: Hay House Inc., 2002.

Hicks, Jerry and Esther Hicks (The Teachings of Abraham). *Money and the Law of Attraction: Learning to Attract Wealth, Health, and Happiness.* Carlsbad, Calif.: Hay House Inc., 2008.

Hicks, Jerry and Esther Hicks. *Ask and It Is Given: Learning to Manifest Your Desires.* Carlsbad, Calif.: Hay House Inc., 2004.

Icke, David. *The David Icke Guide to the Global Conspiracy* (and how to end it). Isle of Wight, UK: David Icke Books Ltd., 2007.

Lipton, Bruce. *The Biology of Belief: Unleashing the Power of Consciousness, Matter and Miracles.* Santa Rosa, Calif.: Mountain of Love/Elite Books, 2005.

Millman, Dan. *The Way of the Peaceful Warrior: A Book That Changes Lives.* Tiburon, Calif., H. J. Kramer and New World Library, 2000.

Crane, Lawrence. *The Abundance Course*, Lawrence Crane Enterprises, 1998

http://www.practical-personal-development-advice.com/lawofattraction.html

http://www.heartmath.org/research/research-home/coherence.html?submenuheader=0

Recommended Reading:

These books I have found to be excellent and I highly recommend them. They are in no particular order. Select the ones that you feel attracted to you as they will probably be ones that provide something you are looking for. There are many more that are not on this list but this is a good start.

The Divine Matrix by Gregg Braden

The Power of Intention by Dr. Wayne Dyer

Ask and It is Given by Jerry and Esther Hicks

You Can Heal Your Life by Louise Hay

Matrix Energetics by Richard Bartlett, DC, ND

Journey of Souls by Michael Newton Ph.D.

Destiny of Souls by Michael Newton Ph.D.

Money and the Law of Attraction by Esther and Jerry Hicks

The True Power of Water by Masaru Emoto

The Hidden Messages in Water by Masaru Emoto

The Source Field Investigations by David Wilcock

The Amazing Power of Deliberate Intent by Esther Hicks and Jerry Hicks

www.ingramcontent.com/pod-product-compliance
Lightning Source LLC
Chambersburg PA
CBHW021054090426
42738CB00006B/341